Learn to Play Guitar

akismet

IN 24 HOURS

D0491831

© 2010 Omnibus Press
(A Division of Music Sales Ltd)
14-15 Berners Street, London W1T 3LJ, UK.

Exclusive Distributors:
Music Sales Limited
Distribution Centre, Newmarket Road,
Bury St Edmunds, Suffolk IP33 3YB, UK.
Music Sales Corporation
257 Park Avenue South,
New York, NY10010, USA.
Macmillan Distribution Services
56 Parkwest Drive,
Derrimut Vic 3000,
Australia.

Order No. OP53031
ISBN 978-0-7119-4130-4

Project Editor: David Harrison.
Music processed by Paul Ewers Music Design.
Cover and book design by Fresh Lemon.
DVD mastered by Technote Media.

Printed in the EU.

A catalogue record for this book is
available from the British Library.

Your Guarantee of Quality
As publishers, we strive to produce
every book to the highest commercial standards.
 The music has been freshly engraved and the book
has been carefully designed to minimise awkward
page turns and to make playing from it a real pleasure.
 Particular care has been given to specifying acid-free,
neutral-sized paper made from pulps which have
not been elemental chlorine bleached. This pulp
is from farmed sustainable forests and was produced
with special regard for the environment.
 Throughout, the printing and binding have been
planned to ensure a sturdy, attractive publication
which should give years of enjoyment.
 If your copy fails to meet our high standards,
please inform us and we will gladly replace it.

www.musicsales.com

Learn *to* **Play** Guitar

IN 24 HOURS

David Mead

FOREWORD

Hello, and welcome to Learn Acoustic Guitar In 24 Hours. During the course of these Chapters, and on the DVD itself, we will be showing you how to begin playing the acoustic guitar and I promise to keep all the unnecessary jargon and buzzwords to an absolute minimum.

That was the thing that used to frustrate me when I was learning: I'd often spend hours trying to find out what some arcane musical term I'd just read about actually meant, and usually discover that I didn't need to know it at all! Here we are going to concentrate on making those all-important first steps together as quickly and as efficiently as we can.

There's a lot of ground to cover and I'm sure that you are eager to get on with playing your first few notes, but I'd suggest that you read the sections at the beginning of the book first as they contain a lot of important information about your instrument.

After that, feel free to turn to Chapter 1 and begin the path toward playing. The acoustic guitar is a beautiful instrument and I'm sure you will spend many hours having fun with it. Good luck!

DAVID MEAD, 2008

INTRODUCTION:

00

INTRODUCTION 1: CHOOSING AN ACOUSTIC GUITAR

The chances are that you will be reading this chapter in retrospect as it's unlikely that you would buy a guitar tutor first and a guitar second! So this is likely to be more of a checklist than anything else but, if the guitar works its magic on you in the same way that it has on generations before, there will come a time when you fancy upgrading and buying something a bit special. So read on...

JAMES TAYLOR
American acoustic guitarist and singer-songwriter supremo.

One of the principal differences between 'budget' and 'bespoke' instruments is in the choice of body materials and whether the instrument has been totally handmade or if the various body parts were mass produced as part of an automated process. The most expensive instruments are usually made over a period of months in small workshops using only the finest body woods and first grade accessories like tuning machines, fretwire and so on. It's basically the same as anything; you get what you pay for.

Once upon a time, back in the days when I was learning, it was almost impossible to buy a good acoustic guitar without spending many hundreds of pounds. Back then, a lot of us learnt on instruments that were very poorly made, with very high-playing actions (i.e. the height of the strings above the fretboard was quite daunting, making holding the strings down very difficult indeed) and would now probably be regarded as medieval torture devices.

Luckily, modern manufacturing processes, computer design and other current day wonders have changed things around completely and most of the instruments I've seen recently – even at the budget end of the spectrum – have been of very good quality and totally suitable to learn on.

Here's a brief check list of things to watch out for:

BODY WOODS

Top-of-the-range models usually use either cedar or spruce for the soundboard or 'top' of the guitar. Both are very resilient and straight-grained which all count towards giving the guitar a loud and sweet voice. Remember that the sound of an acoustic guitar isn't just down to one thing, it's a combination of factors all working together.

You may come across the expression *laminated top*, which means that the soundboard of the guitar is basically some nice looking wood pressed onto a cheaper one in a sort of sandwich or *ply*. Many cheaper acoustics have laminated tops and it's not always a bad thing, but the upper range models nearly always have tops made from a single piece of wood and are known as *solid tops*.

The back and sides of quality acoustics are usually made from woods like solid mahogany or rosewood and the manufacturers of the more upper range instruments will often use woods from specific areas, too. In the past, body wood exotica included Brazilian rosewood and Honduras mahogany, but these two woods are now extremely rare as they are both endangered species and stocks are pretty much depleted worldwide. Instead, look

*While many people opt for the classic **dreadnought** body shape, as shown on this Martin, some prefer the increased accessibility to the higher frets afforded by the cutaway feature seen here on the right.*

for Indian rosewood and mahogany sourced from other areas, too, as they are still used in manufacture and give excellent results.

This doesn't mean that all other types of wood are to be disregarded, of course. Many guitar makers will spend years experimenting with different types of wood to very good effect.

As far as neck material is concerned, mahogany is virtually an industry standard, offering strength and durability in the playing area. You may hear guitar publications refer to 'neck profiles' and this is really just the shape the wood is carved into so that it fits nicely into the hollow between your left-hand fingers and thumb. Some players like a 'V' profile, meaning that the shape of the guitar neck's back looks a bit like the letter V when viewed in cross section. Others will talk of 'C' or 'D' profiling and these are really just areas of fine tuning: virtuoso players can be a very fussy bunch when it comes down to the instruments they play!

Fingerboards are nearly always either rosewood or ebony: both hard-working, durable woods that stand up well to all the abuse they receive from fingers and strings. Once again, look out for substitutes here, too; many of the new generation of guitar builders will source fine alternatives in the interest of cost efficiency.

The bridge on the guitar will often be made from rosewood or ebony, too as this is another area that has to be strong and hard wearing.

That's just about it as far as actual woods are concerned. The nut and bridge inserts on guitars today are usually made from plastic at the low end and either bone or a synthetic substitute at the high end.

ELECTRO-ACOUSTIC OR FULL ACOUSTIC?

One of the greatest advances in acoustic guitar technology that has been made over the last 20 years or so is in the way a guitar can now be amplified, just like a solid body electric guitar. In days of yore, the only way an audience was going to be able to hear your acoustic guitar was if you stood stock still on stage with a microphone in front of you. Even then the results weren't always that great. Now, thanks to some very clever science, it is common to find *piezo transducers* hidden away under your bridge's string saddle. These pick up the vibration from the strings, turn them into a minute electrical signal which is then taken to a cunningly concealed pre-amplifier and out of the guitar via a plug which doubles as a strap peg on the bottom of the guitar. This means that you can plug your guitar into an amplifier or PA system and everyone can hear what you're doing, even if you want to run around the stage in the manner of a rock god.

Here again, quality comes into the equation and some of the more elite variations will even sport a microphone hidden inside the guitar's body as well as the under saddle pick-up.

All well and good, of course, if you see yourself performing in front of more than just a couple of people at some point in the future. If the very thought of playing in front of anyone fills you with a phobic-sized dread then the chances are that you'd be better off with a 'full acoustic' which is just modern day music shop parlance for an acoustic guitar without a pick-up.

Is there a difference between the two, other than being able to plug one in and not the other? Well, possibly, yes…

Getting the best acoustic sound out of something that is essentially a wooden box is hard enough at the best of times and builders strive to wring the last drop of tone out of the instruments they build. If you add in the fact that the guitar is meant to deliver a good electric sound as well, things can become altogether more complicated from the point of view of construction. Some concessions have to be made: a slightly thicker top to stop the guitar howling like some denizen of hell every time it's plugged in, for instance, is not uncommon. All this can compromise the optimum build status to the effect that you end up with something that's trying hard to give you the best of both worlds, but not succeeding in quite the same way as it would have done if accentuating its merits as a pure acoustic were the sole objective.

So you can see that it's a decision worth taking seriously, but remember that you can always have a pick-up system added later on if you're suddenly bitten by the fame and stardom bug.

Realistically, your best ally in the guitar-buying arena is a good set of ears, and not necessarily your own, either.

An acoustic guitar sounds better when you hear it from across a room, rather than from a player's perspective. So it is a good idea to take someone with you to the guitar shop to act as a sounding board and test pilot while you make the decision.

The bottom line is always going to be 'if it feels good and sounds good, it's probably the one for you'.

*By the way, just so we're clear: **electro-acoustic** refers to acoustic guitars with in-built pick-ups that amplify the acoustic sound, such as this Washburn cutaway model.*

***Semi-acoustic** is something else altogether: this describes a guitar that is essentially an electric guitar (with surface-mounted pick-ups) but which has a hollow body, providing an acoustic amplification along with the electronic variety. This sunburst Gibson 335 is a semi-acoustic.*

NAMING THE PARTS

In order to navigate around your acoustic guitar more easily, you are going to have to familiarise yourself with some of the terms in common use which are used to describe its various bits and pieces. As you may suspect, in many cases there is more than one name for some of the parts. I'll try to let you know about all the variations as we go, though. Let's start at the top and work down...

To begin with, the very top end of your guitar, where the strings are all anchored, is known as the *headstock*. Mounted on the headstock are the six tuners, sometimes known as *machine heads*. The ends of the strings are wrapped around *capstans* or *tuning pegs*.

The part below the headstock where the strings cross over a bit of white or cream plastic or bone material is known as the *nut*. This is quite important to remember because the nut is one end of the playing area of the string and you'll quite often hear guitarists or teachers talk about playing 'down at the nut end', and now you know where they mean.

Following on down the guitar from the nut we find the *fretboard*: which is the actual playing surface where you place your fingers to play either chords or melodies. The metal bars that go across the fretboard are known as *fretwires* and the chances are that you've got around 20 of them.

The fretboard is the front side of this area – the playing surface – but the bit that your thumb rests upon around the back is known as the *neck*. Sometimes these two terms collide in popular use and you'll hear guitarists refer to their guitar's neck when they do in fact mean the fretboard. Nobody said this was going to be easy, did they?

You might be wondering what the spots on the fretboard and along its side are all about, too. I'm often asked if these actually have any musical significance and the swift answer is 'no, not really'. The fact is that they are there to aid navigation: you'll soon learn that they feature at the third, fifth, seventh, ninth, 12th, 15th, 17th and 19th frets, and this helps you line things up visually (hence the name, *fret markers*). However, variations abound and you may find that your particular model of acoustic guitar has fewer or more, but it's really down to individual design.

The chances are that your guitar's fretboard joins the body of the instrument at the 14th fret. It's virtually an industry standard with acoustics, although some makes and models join the body at the 12th instead. It doesn't make too much difference, although the models that have the joint around fret 14 mean that you can play further up the neck without your left-hand fingers colliding with the body or having to do anything athletic with your thumb.

If you turn your guitar over on its back and look at the place where the neck joins the body, you'll probably see a lump of carved wood where the back of the neck has been given a larger surface area to make a more secure fit onto the body. This is known as the *heel* and marks the outside evidence of the cunning carpentry that is holding these two parts of the instrument together. Obviously this has to be quite a strong joint as the neck is constantly under tension from the strings.

The body of the guitar has three main areas: front, back and sides. It's pretty obvious where you'll find each of these so I'm sure I don't need to go into too much detail here.

Mounted about three quarters of the way down the body is the other anchoring point for the guitar strings, known as the *bridge*. The piece of plastic or bone that sits atop the bridge where the strings actually cross before

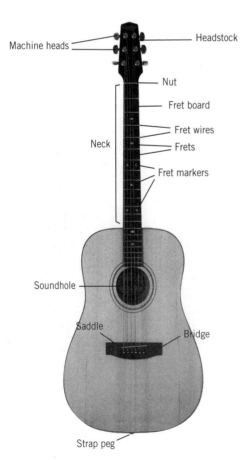

Machine heads — Headstock

Nut

Fret board

Fret wires

Neck — Frets

Fret markers

Soundhole

Saddle

Bridge

Strap peg

disappearing inside is known as the *saddle* or, less commonly, the *bridge bone*. In common parlance, though, we usually say that the playing area of the strings starts at the nut and finishes at the bridge.

Sitting behind the string saddle, you are likely to find six plastic buttons, known as *string pegs*. Please don't fiddle with them quite yet as they are wedging the strings in place and your curiosity might be rewarded with one of them becoming unseated, causing the string to pop out. However, under normal playing conditions everything will remain fixed in place so don't worry.

Just in front of the bridge is a hole, known as the *sound hole* because this is where the sound comes out, unleashing your music onto the world at large. Most of them are round, but I've seen some whacky designs so don't be too surprised if yours is slightly different. It will perform the same kind of job.

Right at the end of the guitar, at its lowest edge, you'll find a metal or plastic button which is called a *strap peg*: this is where you attach one end of your guitar strap. Now a lot of people ask where you attach the other end, and this isn't quite as straightforward.

Years ago, acoustic guitarists who were brave enough to stand up to perform had to tie the other end of their guitar strap around the headstock of the guitar with

something resembling a shoelace. If you check back at some pictures, particularly from the acknowledged rock 'n' roll era during the 1950s, you will see plenty of evidence of this technique. Today, however, a lot of guitarists feel far more secure if they are able to attach the other end of their strap to the guitar's body, rather than the neck's extremities. This isn't such an easy job because the sides and back of a guitar are actually quite thin so drilling into them in the hope of attaching a load-bearing strap button usually ends in tragedy. So, remember me telling you about the heel of the guitar neck? This is a piece of wood that is usually thick enough to drill into and so many strap buttons are 'retro-fitted' here. It's certainly not a job for the faint-hearted or the enthusiastic amateur wielding an electric drill, though, so if you decide you need another anchoring point for your strap and the manufacturer hasn't provided one, go and see a specialist guitar technician and get it done safely.

I've covered all of the important bits and pieces which go together to make up an acoustic guitar. Obviously there are some I've missed out because of space or because some parts of the guitar have three or four names and I didn't want to confuse you unnecessarily. You'll hear talk of *upper bouts and lower bouts, purfling, kerfing and X bracing* among the guitar's cognoscenti, but these really needn't bother you now.

PAUL WELLER
Both Weller's '70s group The Jam and his '80s project, Style Council, received great critical acclaim and had a huge influence on the 1990's generation of UK guitar bands.

POSTURE

Learning any instrument carries with it certain demands of the physique of the player. In the classical world, for instance, posture is something that is taken very seriously indeed, to the extent that many teachers insist that there is, in fact, only one way to hold, sit with and play the instrument concerned. Classical guitarists are nearly always to be found sitting on straight-backed chairs with their left foot raised on a special stool with the guitar's headstock level with their shoulders. Hand positions on classical guitar are quite defined, too; the left-hand thumb sits squarely at the back of the guitar neck in as central a position as possible to ensure that all four fretting fingers have maximum reach across the fretboard. The right hand hovers in space slightly to the back of the guitar's sound hole with the wrist slightly curved. See what I mean about posture being taken seriously in the classical guitar world?

Of course, rock 'n' roll means tearing up the rule book so there aren't the same kind of strictures in place when it comes down to learning acoustic guitar. But, while videos and television performances by modern day acoustic troubadours would seem to imply that virtually anything goes in terms of posture, there are a few recommendations you'd be well advised to take on board.

To begin with, there is a certain element of health & safety in the workplace to be taken into consideration when playing an acoustic. It may sound mad, but when you think about it, the human body wasn't really designed with guitar playing in mind. We do ask an awful lot of our arms, wrists, hands and fingers, and they endure a lot of strain, too, in much the same way that an athlete or gymnast uses every ounce of muscle power available to them. Luckily for us, we don't have to think about training for a marathon, but we're still talking about muscles, tendons and other biological factors that come in to play while we idly strum the night away.

The point I'm making is that you can expect certain muscles in your hands to be very weak and almost uncontrollable to begin with, and I'm asking you to be very patient while nature takes its course in this respect. Certain things might seem 'impossible' to begin with, but given a little time and a lot of practice

will begin to feel easier as we progress. So every time you're tempted to wimp out because something I've asked you to do seems really awkward and unwieldy remember that all that's probably happening is that nature has still to play a game of catch up and it's well within your power to bring all of your abilities as a guitarist on line with a little work.

As far as defining the posture and practice habits that are advisable to adopt, here are a few guidelines:

Classical guitarists adopt strict technique in posture and hand positions

SITTING WITH THE GUITAR

It really is advisable to sit on a chair to practise, and while this might sound like something really obvious to say, you'd be surprised how many people try to put some time in with their guitars while slouched on a sofa or armchair. Try to sit with your back as straight as possible, too; and don't be tempted to curve your back or crane your neck to see what's going on with your fingers. Both of these will give you some aches and pains you really don't deserve in the short term, and set up some bad habits for the future while you're at it.

AVOID TENSION

A lot of beginners worry that their guitar is going to slip off their lap and tend to grip it tightly, which really only has the effect of tensing the muscles that we are trying to use. If you feel clumsy and unfamiliar with holding the guitar to begin with, try wearing a guitar strap. It's a fail-safe mechanism for keeping the guitar in approximately the right position and you definitely won't be in danger of dropping it. Above everything, try to relax with the guitar. You are meant to work together and not fight one another, after all.

Non-classical acoustic guitarists are less bound by tradition and technique...

...but should always aim for comfort and avoid undue strain

NO DISTRACTIONS

Try to find somewhere quiet to practise. I know this is a very difficult thing to do in the maelstrom of modern domestic life, but it's important that you focus on the various tasks within the lessons and unwanted background noise is an important thing to avoid.

Practising with the television on in the background is an absolute no! In order to progress quickly in these all-important initial stages you need to be as free as possible from both audio and visual pollutants; and the TV is the worst thing for both.

STAY REGULAR

It is helpful if you try to allocate the same time every day to do your practice. By doing so, it helps guitar playing become part of a daily routine, making it easier to plan around and harder to avoid. With my busier pupils in the past I have found that designating, say, 8–8.30pm every evening for practice actually helps them progress.
It's just like having a set time to visit a gym: you tend to be more disciplined than you would do if it was more of a case of *open all hours* flexibility.

DON'T OVERDO THINGS

Of course, I wouldn't dream of curbing anyone's enthusiasm for practice, but it's not a wise thing to go for overkill, particularly with some of the tougher physical manoeuvres you have to ask your body to do in the early stages. Everyone has heard of repetitive strain injury, but tend to associate it with things like typing or operating machinery. Well, the fact is that guitarists are prone to it, too, and over-practice and bad posture are two of the principal causes.

I am not going to give you a biology lesson, but your fingers, wrists and so on are all operated by a complex array of muscles and tendons, and these are prone to damage if we don't take due care. At every point of the way, take a good look at what you're asking your body to do and if it involves folding your hand over at a right angle with your arm, the chances are you're not doing it right. Stop, think about it and try adjusting your position to make things easier for all the biological machinery that's working away under the surface. Take heed of all this advice and things should go well for you, but remember: there's no such thing as 'good pain' as far as guitar playing is concerned and you would therefore be very wise to seek medical assistance at the first sign of any undue discomfort.

You will get a good idea about the dos and don'ts of posture from watching the accompanying DVD. We cover hand and arm position right at the start, so if you're in any doubt at all, check back with Chapter 1 and make sure everything is in order.

TUNING

To say that your instrument was 'in tune when I bought it' is a favourite joke among guitarists. Even if it was in tune back at the shop it almost certainly won't have been when you got it home. Guitars go out of tune quite easily and for many different reasons – even atmospheric conditions can have an affect on tuning stability – so it's something that we all have to deal with every day of our playing lives.

In fact, tuning should be your first job every time you sit down with your guitar to practise as playing anything on a badly-tuned instrument doesn't do you any good at all. Part of learning to be a musician involves developing your ear, and ears are trained in much the same way that muscles are developed in a gym. It takes time, patience and a lot of practice, but eventually your ears will begin to develop along with your playing and the two will work side-by-side, making you a better all-round musician.

All this aside, how are we going to tackle the tricky task of tuning? My advice here is to buy an electronic tuner as this will definitely save you an awful lot of angst in these initial stages. Basically, all electronic tuners work in the same way: most of the acoustic guitar tuners on the market have some sort of microphone built into them so you set it up in front of your guitar, play an open string and let the tuner tell you if it's in tune or not.

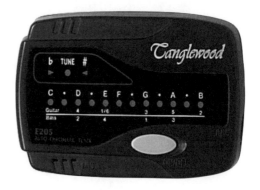

If this sounds a little like kindergarten to you, rest assured that even top professionals tune their instruments this way as it's very accurate and fast.

Of course, there is a way that you can tune by ear, but it does depend on how good you are at sensing if two strings are playing the same pitch. If you pick up your guitar and play the note at the fifth fret on the bass E string, it should sound the same as its next door neighbour, the A string:

The guitar is tuned like this:

E A D G B E

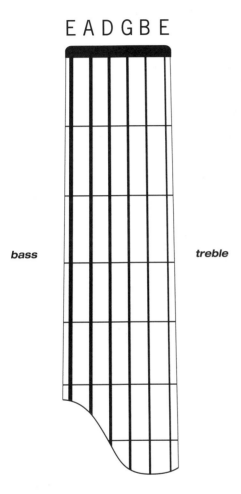

bass   **treble**

E A D G B E

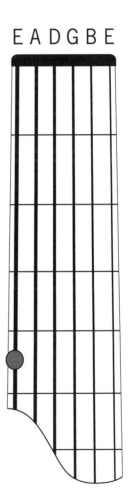

So if you play your bass E string into the tuner, it will say if it's tuned too high (which we call *sharp*) or tuned too low (which we call *flat*). If it's too low, you merely turn your tuning peg on the guitar a little in an anti-clockwise direction (not too far, they're pretty sensitive) until the tuner tells you you're spot on. If your E string is tuned too high, you lower it slightly by turning the tuning peg in a clockwise direction.

Sounds easy enough, doesn't it? All you have to do then is repeat the process for all six strings and then go back and do a quick check (i.e. play each string again just to make sure it hasn't moved since you tuned it the first time) and you're ready to practise or play.

If it doesn't, it will once again be either sharp (too high) or flat (too low) and you'll need to adjust the tuning peg as before. This 'quick check' method of tuning works right across the guitar until you reach the G and B strings. This time, if you play the G string at the fourth fret, it sounds the same as the B:

When you want to see if the top two strings – the B and E – are in tune, you return once again to the fifth fret:

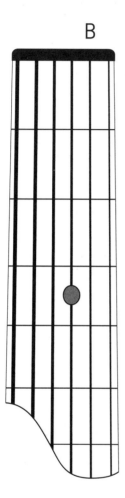

B

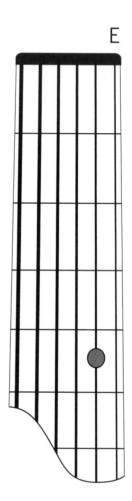

E

Now this method might look simple, and it's certainly as quick as the electronic tuner method, but it's usually not quite so accurate. Even a good musical ear can be 'out' by as much as ten per cent when trying to tune this way so, if you start tuning from the bass side and add in a compound error across all six strings, you can be well and truly out of whack by the time you reach the B and E strings.

So it is a better idea to get hold of an electronic tuner and keep it in your guitar case at all times. It is quick, simple and deadly accurate, and means you can spend more time practising, too.

UPKEEP

Any instrument requires a certain amount of care and attention to keep it in good shape. Remember, we're not just talking about the occasional polish to keep it shiny, a guitar is a precision instrument and will give you years of trouble-free service as long as you look after it by following some common-sense rules.

PUT IT AWAY

It is rare to buy a guitar now that doesn't come with some sort of case, even if it's a soft cover or *gig bag* as they're sometimes called. The fact is that even a soft case is better than nothing at all as it encourages you to put it away after a practice or playing session and keep it somewhere out of harm's way. We're all aware of the stampede that is modern day domestic living and I've seen instruments damaged by the family pet having a loony five minutes and knocking the thing over.

The more expensive instruments come with a hard case which come in all shapes and sizes ranging from the type made from what is essentially super stiff cardboard to the luxury class that you could safely drive a tank over.

The fact is that guitars can become dented, scratched or worse quite easily, so some kind of case is the best kind of insurance you can buy.

KEEP IT CLEAN

Not surprisingly, guitars are prone to accumulating dust and grime the same as anything you keep around the house. Dust and fingerprints are easily dealt with by using a duster and some household furniture polish (although it's generally a good idea to avoid the types that include silicone in their formula because it can get on the strings and cause problems). But the most important area to keep clean is the playing area itself, meaning the strings and fretboard. You don't need to become fanatical about this as a quick wipe down with a dry cloth after a playing session is usually all that's needed. You'll probably be surprised at how quickly the strings can pick up grime – sweaty fingers leave a moist bloom on the metal and this attracts dust and dirt – and dirty strings don't sound too good.

Pro Tip: getting dust out from under the strings on the headstock and top of the guitar is much easier if you use a clean one-inch paintbrush!

DON'T OVERHEAT

This is a case of common sense, but acoustic guitars are made from wood held together by glue. Neither of these like undue heat and humidity. For most of us who don't live in a tropical region this doesn't sound like too much of a problem, but central heating, open fires, portable heaters, direct sunlight, parked cars and so on can all contribute to a very unhealthy atmosphere for your guitar if it's left too close. So, as a general rule of thumb, think twice about leaving your instrument leaning up against a radiator or in bright sunlight and all should be well.

DON'T STACK

This is another area of common sense, but an acoustic guitar is basically a box and the soundboard (or top) of the guitar is usually made from quite thin wood (to help it vibrate and produce that beautiful music you're going to be playing). So, if you're packing up to go on holiday and want to take a guitar with you, think about where you're going to put it.

STRINGS

As you can probably imagine, 'how often do I need to change my strings?' is the all-time winner in the guitarist's Frequently Asked Questions stakes. Without a doubt, strings are going to be your greatest ongoing expense, but the answer to the question is possibly a little bit more involved than you might think.

When you buy a fresh set of strings, they are clean, shiny and perfectly round in shape. After a few weeks of heavy practising they begin to become tarnished, mucky and all that bashing against the frets has altered their shape a little. Take a good look at a set of worn strings and you'll be able to see grooves where the frets have dented them. If you can't actually see them, try running your finger along the underside of the string and you should definitely be able to feel ridges along its length. All this can have an effect on the sound of the string, usually showing up firstly as a loss in treble or *brightness*. Factor in metal fatigue from being stretched under tension (on average this can easily clock in at 20lbs) and being generally bashed about in the interests of music making and you've got some very unhealthy strings!

One of the reasons why there is no straight answer to the question of how often strings should be changed is that it tends to be different from person to person, player to player. If you practise often and play 'hard' then you're obviously going to wear a set of strings out sooner than someone who practises less frequently and has a much lighter touch. Even body chemistry can have an effect on strings, though: sweat is basically a corrosive element and you'll find your strings tarnishing much quicker if you sweat a lot when you play.

Modern science has come to our aid a little here and now some companies are offering strings that have been coated with an anti-corrosive agent which helps prolong their serviceable life. I use this type of string on my acoustic guitars and they do actually work as I find that I need to change my strings far less often than before.

A professional guitarist will change his strings well before they reach the end of their tonal life. You can bet that most guitarists you see live and hear on recordings will be playing on a fresh set of strings, too, as this is a way of keeping a predictable enough level of consistency to their sound. The good news is that you have to fall somewhere in between: you don't need to be as obsessive as a pro player about it (many of whom get their strings either free or much cheaper than you can buy them in the shops, anyway) but you certainly won't be doing yourself any favours by keeping them on well past the time when their useful life is over. Worn strings are difficult to tune and are liable to break so changing them at sensible intervals is the best discipline to engage.

Meanwhile, remember that a good wipe down with a clean cloth after practising will do wonders in preserving string life, too.

As far as your first string change is concerned, I would advise you to find someone who has some previous experience to do it for you while you watch. As with anything, it's really not that hard but there is definitely a knack to it, so if you know anyone who has been playing for a while, or if there is a sympathetic soul at your local friendly guitar store, it is well worth paying whatever it costs you for a quick lesson in string changing.

One final word on guitar string: don't be tempted by cheap strings. Look for a make you've heard of or do some research on the internet or in a guitar magazine to find out what other players use and recommend. Cheap strings usually aren't made that well and can cause you problems. Beware!

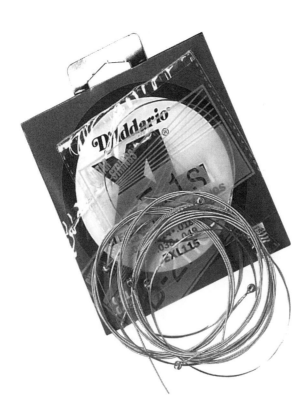

GOAL: TO ACCLIMATISE YOURSELF TO SITTING AND HOLDING THE INSTRUMENT, AND LEARNING YOUR FIRST CHORD AND RHYTHM PATTERN.

FIRST THINGS FIRST

Before you do anything else, make sure that you're in tune. I've gone through the basics in the section on tuning and have stressed the importance of practising on a perfectly tuned instrument there. At this stage, your ears won't recognise whether the guitar is exactly in pitch or not, so I'm hoping that you took my advice and bought an electronic tuner. If not, do your best via the other method I describe and try to be as accurate as you can.

It would be helpful if you read the section on naming the guitar's various bits and pieces before we begin, too. You'll pick up all of the main navigation points quickly enough, but a little bit of initial spade work in this respect will still prove worthwhile.

WORKOUTS

Now, I'd recommend that you find a quiet place and a straight-back chair, and pick up your guitar. To begin with you're going to feel really awkward holding the instrument on your lap – it's inevitable that there will be a settling-in phase to go through – and it's a good idea to move around slowly if you're walking with it from room to room. I've seen a lot of inadvertent damage done to instruments simply from walking through doors or downstairs.

Eventually, you won't even have to think about the extra bulk, length and general dimension of your guitar, but for now it's best to think of yourself as a 'wide load' when on the move.

One more thing before we start: as you sit and hold the guitar, the string that is nearest your face – the thick bass string – is known in guitar circles as the *bottom string* and its thin counterpart which is nearest the floor is known as the *top string*. I know this seems the wrong way around, but the strings get their name from the fact that they are the lowest and highest in pitch and not from their actual physical position. It's a small point, but I've known it to cause an awful lot of confusion during lessons.

WORKOUT 1

The very first thing we're going to do is play a chord called E minor. It's one of the easier chords and a good place to start. You will need to look at the diagram below before moving any further:

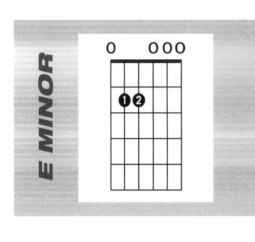

This is what is known as a chord box and you have to imagine you are looking at your guitar's fretboard straight on, with the bass string on the left and the top string on the right. The marks on the fingerboard represent where you are going to put your fingers and, seeing as all of this is new to you, we're going to place the fingers one at a time.

Firstly, let's put a system in place for numbering your left-hand fingers. We're going to go out from the thumb so your index finger will be 'one', your middle finger 'two' and so on. For the chord of E minor, you will be needing fingers one and two.

On the DVD we show you how to position the fingers and make sure that all the strings are ringing clearly. Take a look at Chapter 1 to find out the exact method for playing E minor correctly.

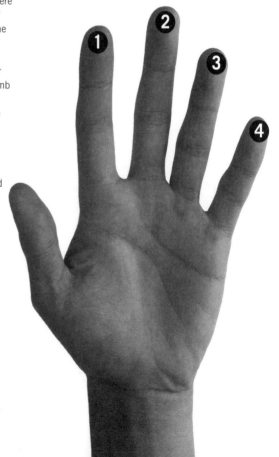

WORKOUT 2

The next thing we're going to do is learn how to strum the chord using the right hand. At the moment it doesn't really matter if you choose to use a plectrum or your fingers to strike the strings. We can worry about fine tuning your technique later on. For now, all we want to do is hear the chord.

If you play four consecutive downstrokes on your E minor chord, remembering not to 'push' the strings too much, it will sound like it does on the recording.

In music, songs are split into small chunks called 'bars' and they usually have four beats in them. Beats are the 'pulse' within music – the basic element of rhythm – so, as you play, it's a good idea to count aloud '1 2 3 4' so that you know where you are. I know you'll feel a complete idiot doing this, but trust me, it's important.

E minor

1   2   3   4   1   2   3   4

PERFORMANCE PIECE

Your goal for this Chapter is to be able to play the E minor chord correctly – and, if possible, from memory – and play the two bars of four downstrokes, counting as you play.

E minor

1   2   3   4   1   2   3   4   1   2   3   4   1   2   3   4

SUMMARY

Congratulations, you have just played some music on your guitar.
Keep checking that every note is clear every so often and run through the finger position checklist we've outlined on the DVD if you come across any buzzes or muted strings.

GOAL: LOOKING AT A COUPLE MORE CHORDS TO ADD A LITTLE VARIETY TO YOUR PRACTICE TIME. STUDYING AN ALTERNATIVE TO THE DOWNSTROKE STRUM PATTERN.

MORE CHORDS

To begin with, remember to check your tuning. I promise I won't remind you again, but it is important to make tuning a habit as playing anything on an out of tune guitar isn't good for your ears.

WORKOUT 1

The next chord to look at is A minor. Here it is as a diagram:

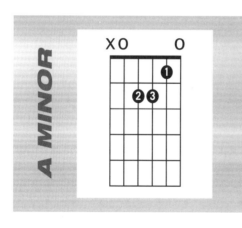

You will see that this time we'll be using three fingers and that they are all together in a bunch. Take a look at the DVD and let us talk you through positioning your fingers.

WORKOUT 2

Our next chord is D minor and here it is in chord box form:

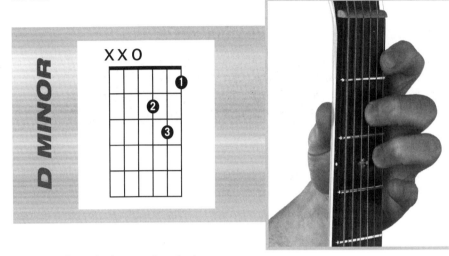

D MINOR

X X O

It is a three-finger chord once again and we've gone through how to position your digits on the DVD, so take a look.

WORKOUT 3

The new chords I've introduced here will prove to be a bit of a workout for the left hand, but what about the right? In Chapter 1 we learned how to strike the strings downwards 'four to the bar' so this time we're going to be looking at things the other way around and learn to play an *upstroke*.

In a perfect world, upstrokes would feel and sound exactly like their downstroke counterparts, but this isn't really the case. It's quite difficult to get consecutive up and downstrokes sounding even, but it's an important part of rhythm playing to be able to pull this one off.

I'd recommend that you begin practising your upstroke using the E minor chord as you might not have to worry too much about what your left hand is doing and give yourself the opportunity to focus on the right.

Have a few experimental stabs at playing an upstroke so that you can judge the exact amount of force that you need to put into the strings, and watch the DVD section for guidance.

PERFORMANCE PIECE

Once you have something that sounds good, practice playing a downstroke followed by an upstroke and count it like this:

The '1 2 3 4' should all be downstrokes and the 'ands' should all be upstrokes. Try playing the three chords you know using alternate down and upstrokes, like this:

E minor

A minor

D minor

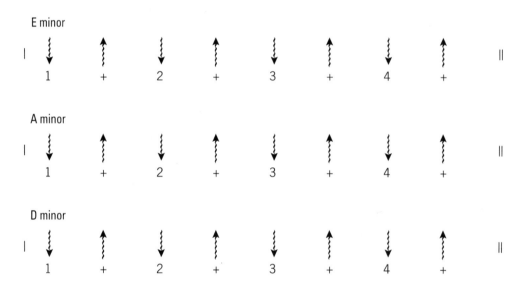

Play through these three examples separately: don't try to join things up for the moment because that comes later on and there are special techniques to learn first. Just concentrate in getting a good, even rhythm sound – maybe using a click like the one on the DVD – and we'll join things up later on.

SUMMARY

Building a chord vocabulary is essential in the early days of playing guitar. You'll be using chords all your playing life and it's never too soon to start. Rhythm is vitally important too. Obviously there is a lot more to it than just simple up and downstrokes, but getting these basics right now will enable you to build on your knowledge later on.

GOAL: *LOOKING AT AND LEARNING MORE CHORDS.*

CHORD FAMILIES

By now, I hope your practising is settling into a daily routine. As I said in the beginning, we can't expect rampant progress in these early days, but there is an awful lot that only regular repetition can achieve. You're doubtless finding that the fingers on both hands are slow to respond, clumsy and awkward, and the guitar itself probably still feels unnatural on your lap. But all these things can and will be ironed out with a little patience and perseverance, I assure you. So if you're finding that the chords we've looked at so

far still don't sound 100 per cent right when you play them, don't worry too much. Just keep up the regular practice sessions and all will be well.

NB: Understanding the differences between the three different chord families is vitally important for the work we'll be doing in later Chapters. So far, we've looked at chords from a single family: the minor chords. In music, there are basically three different types of chord: minor, major and dominant seventh. Don't worry about the names just yet, these will be explained in time, but we can just take a brief glimpse at the job a couple of them do.

WORKOUT 1

Major and minor chords are opposites: in much the same way that we have sweet & sour and night & day, we have major & minor. Minor chords tend to sound very sad and downcast, but their major counterparts sound quite upbeat and full of energy by comparison. Play through each of the three chords we've learned:

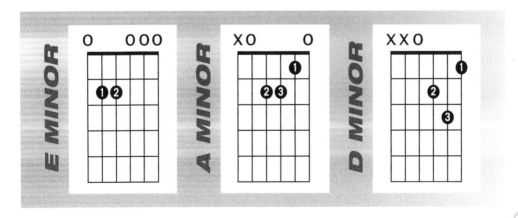

WORKOUT 2

And now, let's look at their major counterparts.
Firstly, here's E major:

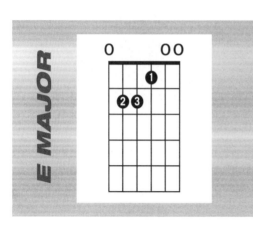

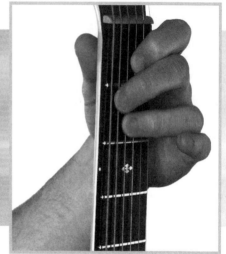

As you can see, there is only a very slight difference
between the major and minor versions of this chord.
Notice how, by simply lifting your left-hand index finger,
you're playing E minor. For this reason, you should aim
to play the E minor chord with the second and third
fingers from now on.

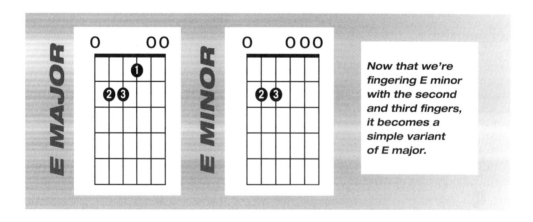

*Now that we're
fingering E minor
with the second
and third fingers,
it becomes a
simple variant
of E major.*

WORKOUT 3

Next, here's D major:

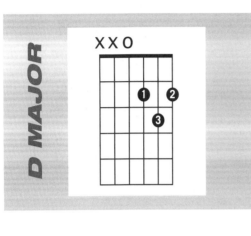 

D MAJOR

Once again, there's only one finger involved in making the change between major and minor versions. D major involves a different fingering, so you'll have to build up some 'finger memory' by repeating these new chords every day for a while.

WORKOUT 4

Lastly, let's look at A major. As you can see, the 'one finger makes all the difference' rule applies here, too, but it's now a bit of a crush at the second fret, with all three left-hand fingers vying for space. Take your time here, getting a good clear note out of each string is going to prove difficult at first with the A major chord, but if you make some patient adjustments each time, you'll find the optimum position where all five strings that are in play ring out cleanly.

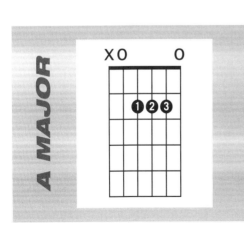 

A MAJOR

PERFORMANCE PIECE

Your target for this Chapter is to play all six chords that you now know in our 'four to the bar' and 'eight to the bar' strumming rhythms, like this:

SUMMARY

In this Chapter we have mentioned the three basic chord families, and we've learned some more shapes, too.
In addition, we're beginning to understand rhythm, employing up and downstrokes in preparation for making song accompaniments sound more interesting.

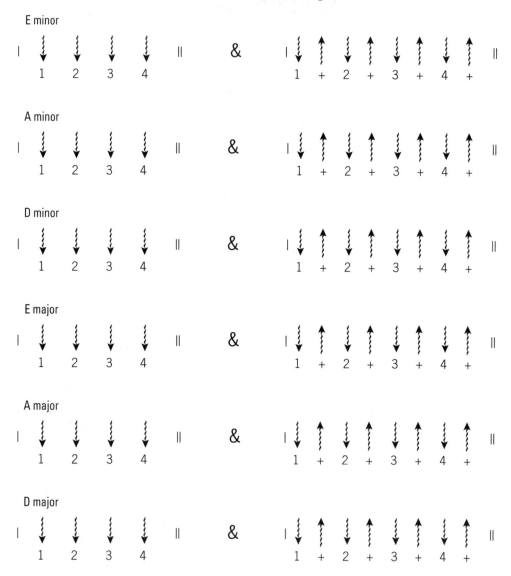

CHAPTER: 04

GOAL: *CHANGING SMOOTHLY BETWEEN CHORDS.*

CHANGING CHORDS

Playing through chords one at a time is all very well, of course: you have as much time as you like to change between them, after all. But if you're playing through a song, the chords can come thick and fast so we're going to have to find a way to change between chords quickly and, more importantly, accurately.

This is another area of 'early learning' on the guitar that can frustrate players as changing chords appears very awkward to begin with: fumbling fingers that never seem to want to do what you tell them. Buzzes, muted strings and so on can all add to the frustration. But let's think about it: you're asking your fingers to do a lot of new and unfamiliar things and the chances are that your left hand in particular has never really been called upon to do anything more technical than hold a cup before now. So let's give those fingers a chance during these initial stages and consider that every guitarist out there has been at this stage at one time or another in his or her playing career, and all of them got through it, so you will, too.

GEM ARCHER
Oasis's rhythm guitarist also often takes lead duties when the band performs live. Gem first found success with Heavy Stereo, who he left to join Oasis, and has also contributed to the recordings of Nine Inch Nails.

WORKOUT 1

Before we look closer at how to move between the chords we have already learned, let's consider the first rule of chord changes:

You always change chords in the air and *never* on the fretboard.

The first time you change between, say, A minor and D minor, there will probably be a temptation to place each finger of the new chord down individually onto the fretboard: but this is entirely the wrong approach. Believe me; you'll save yourself an awful lot of time in the future if you learn to change the chord shape about an inch or so above the fretboard. Ideally, your fingers should be able to drop into position all at once, and you'll see why this is so important in a minute.

Meanwhile, we show you on the DVD what we mean by the aerial ballet you need to master before you can change chords efficiently on the guitar neck.

In order to put all this to the test and to give you something new to practise, we're going to look at our first simple song.

To begin with, we've been playing the chords we've learned *four to the bar* as individual units. Now we're going to string a few of them together.

Just in case your memory is still a bit fuzzy on the chord shapes we've looked at, here they are again, so you won't need to keep looking back in the book:

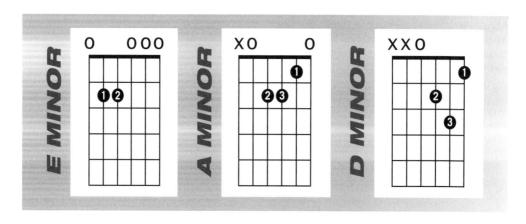

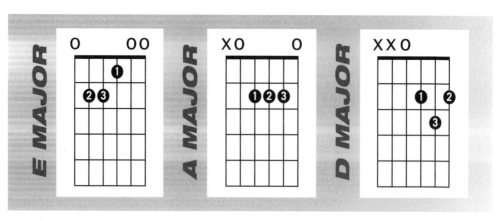

So let's take each chord change individually and learn
how to change between them.

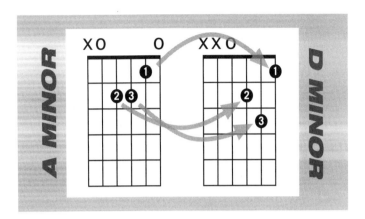

Here's the A minor to D minor. It's a question of quick,
efficient dispersal of fingers one, two and three onto
the fretboard. Don't plant the fingers individually.
Remember: try to form the chord in the space above
the fretboard and go for a perfectly co-ordinated,
simultaneous landing.

WORKOUT 2

Now it's the turn of the D minor to E minor chord
change. Remember to use the updated fingering for
E minor.

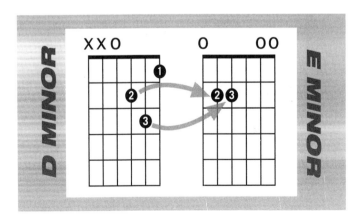

Once again, it's down to careful, well thought
out planning in order to carry out the necessary
choreography.

WORKOUT 3

And now the E minor to A minor. This one doesn't pose the same kind of problem as two of the fingers can stay in formation while they move.

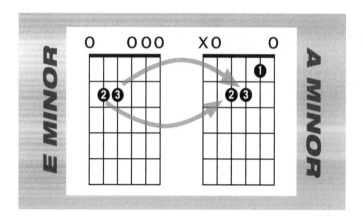

PERFORMANCE PIECE

Here is the chord arrangement for the song:

A minor				D minor				E minor				A minor			
1	2	3	4	1	2	3	4	1	2	3	4	1	2	3	4

I have used the chords that your fingers will be most used to for this first song, but keep on practising the new chords from the last Chapter because we're going to be needing them soon.

SUMMARY

Learning the necessary 'finger skills' to move adroitly between chords is a job worth taking time over as you'll be needing it for your entire playing career. Making sure the spadework is done well here will set you up perfectly for the future.

Follow the DVD for advice on 'economic movement' between chord shapes and try to make sure that each of them change exactly on the first '1' of the bar. It will be slow going for the first few plays through, but keep up the practice routine and you'll find it becoming easier and easier before too long.

GOAL: TO RATIONALISE THE CHORDS THAT WE LEARN, ENSURING THAT THEY ARE DEALT WITH EFFICIENTLY AND PLAYED IN THE MOST ECONOMICAL WAY POSSIBLE.

DOING THE MATHS

By this time you're probably asking yourself the question, 'Well, how many chords are there to learn?' So I thought a little maths might be in order...

In music, there are essentially 12 different notes, repeated over and over again from sub-woofer rumblingly low to bats-only high. The human range of hearing dictates that we can hear about ten or so repeats of the series. Below a certain pitch and we can only detect vibration, and at the top end we're simply not biologically equipped to hear them.

Music obviously operates within our usable hearing zone and if you can imagine the keyboard of a grand piano, then that's about as graphic a layout of the notes in use that you can get.

Naturally, these notes have names and, in the main, are represented by the first seven letters of the alphabet:

A B C D E F G

If we can go back to thinking about a piano keyboard for a couple of seconds, the notes above would represent the white keys, and like I say, they are repeated from low down to high up. The black keys are identified by using the same set of alphabetical reference points, but in order to make their positions within the system as clear as possible, we employ two signs.

This one is known to its friends as a 'flat' sign:

♭

And this one, called a 'sharp':

♯

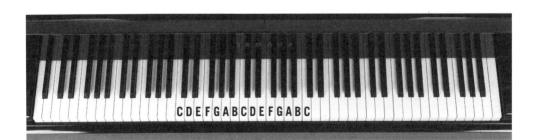

So if we put everything in its place, we arrive at music's master scale, known as the chromatic scale:

A, (A♯/B♭), B, C, (C♯/D♭), D, (D♯E♭), E, F, (F♯/G♭), G, (G♯/A♭)

Now you'll have noticed straight away that there are more than 12 names here, and what are all the brackets about, too? Well, sorry to have to break it to you but some notes in music have two names. It's insane, I know, but it's a system that has been in place in music for a few hundred years so we're pretty much stuck with it. We just have to work around it and try not to let it ruin our day. I will add that if you ever find yourself in conversation with another musician and you say 'B♭' he will know that you're talking about 'A♯' as well.

So what we have with our 'master scale' is the names of all the notes that lie along your A string: that's the second thickest, if you're still not quite sure. If you count along the string, you will find that there are 12 frets before you reach a double dot: that's where the chromatic scale starts all over again.

Now, I realise that all this might seem a lot to take in for now, but it is important that you know about some of this as it will definitely help you orientate yourself across music's often weird terrain.

Getting back to the question about numbers of chords, though, now we know that there are 12 notes in music and three main families of chords, the sum is quite an easy one to work out:

3 x 12 = 36

WORKOUTS

So the basic pack of chords you need to get under your fingers checks in around 36. Not too many, but a lot more than you want to try to cope with all at once. Here are some more to get acquainted with. Once again, there's a theme continuing here.

WORKOUT 1

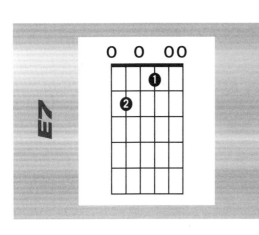

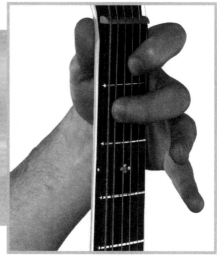

WORKOUT 2

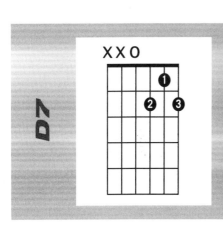

WORKOUT 3

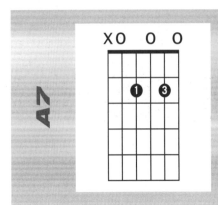

A7

XO   O   O

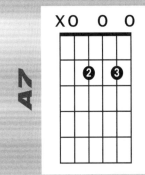

A7

XO   O   O

By the way: the above version of A7 shows how it can be played as a simple variant of A major. In fact, many guitarists end up playing A7 this way, as it's more comfortable.
As soon as you get used to the shape, try to remember this fingering: this is how it will appear for the remainder of this book.

PERFORMANCE PIECE

You are probably getting a little tired of the song from the last Chapter so here's another one. The same rules apply: economical chord changes on the beat, if you please (see DVD).

SUMMARY

Don't allow yourself to be put off by the amount of work there is yet to do as far as chords are concerned. The learning curve here appears very steep to begin with, but it soon begins to get easier as your hands warm up and develop.

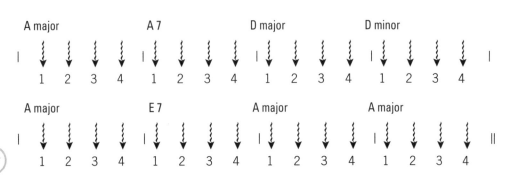

A major	A 7	D major	D minor
1 2 3 4	1 2 3 4	1 2 3 4	1 2 3 4

A major	E 7	A major	A major
1 2 3 4	1 2 3 4	1 2 3 4	1 2 3 4

GOAL: TO LEARN THE BASICS OF GUITAR NOTATION.

*I expect the song exercise from the last
Chapter has kept you busy as it had quite
a few chord changes to it. Don't worry
if it's still not right, there is no need to let
it hold you up. As long as you keep
practising it, things will improve as your
fingers grow more accustomed to
working on the strings.*

In this Chapter we're going to look at something a little
different – the other side of the music coin – melody.
So far we've had a glimpse at how a guitarist
accompanies a song by playing chords with a rhythmic
strum pattern underneath, but there will be times
when you want to play the melody itself on the guitar
and for that we have to learn some new techniques
with both hands.

WORKOUTS

We have to learn another system of notation, too,
but fear not, it's very simple.

Take a look at this:

If you imagine that your guitar is lying flat on the floor
with the headstock to your left and the body to your
right, the diagram above represents the way the strings
are configured. The thick bass E string is at the bottom
and its thin counterpart is on top.

WORKOUT 1

This is a bar of what is known as 'tablature', a very ancient method for writing down melodies for the guitar. If I wanted you to play a note, I would merely tell you which string and fret you would find it on, like this:

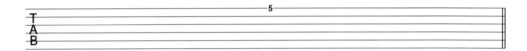

In the tablature above, you would place a left-hand finger on the fifth fret, top E string and pluck it with your right-hand thumb, or any convenient finger, for that matter.

WORKOUT 2

If you haven't invested in a plectrum yet, now is probably a good time. Buy a few (they're only a few pence each) in case you lose one. Try to buy either 'medium' or 'heavy' gauge as anything too thin won't sound too good for playing individual notes.

Hold the pick between the index finger and thumb, like we show you in the DVD. It will feel strange, but you'll soon get used to it. Some players use their fingers to pluck the strings and don't use a pick at all, but it's a good idea for you to consider using one for now and leave making that kind of decision until a bit later on.

Plucking individual notes with a pick is very similar to the idea of strumming chords; there are two movements you can make, a downstroke and an upstroke. As you can see from the DVD, it's economical to use a combination of both: a downstroke, followed by an upstroke. In guitar circles, this is known as 'alternate picking' and has achieved semi-religious status among the more technically minded.

The best way to become used to using a pick is to play exercises like the one below:

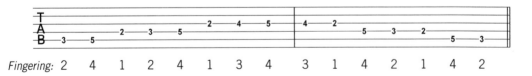

Fingering: 2   4   1   2   4   1   3   4   3   1   4   2   1   4   2

This is a scale of C major which is played on the A, D and G strings of your guitar.

WORKOUT 3

Another way of looking at the same basic information would be this:

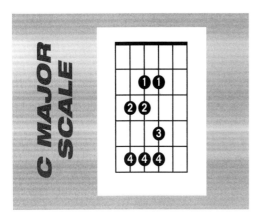

This 'aerial view' of all the notes in the scale on the fretboard at once is known as a *fretboard diagram*. If you use this in conjunction with the tablature, you'll probably have no trouble at all sorting out which notes to play.

PERFORMANCE PIECE

Now you are going to play the scale you have learned over a backing track with a pulse behind it to make sure that everything remains in time.

Fingering: 2   4   1   2   4   1   3   4

Take a good look at how it is played on the DVD and be very self-disciplined with the left-hand fingering as we're beginning to set up good habits here that will stay with you for life.

SUMMARY

In this Chapter we've looked at tablature and fretboard diagrams, and we've learned a scale to play over a backing track. The fundamentals are in place to move further in terms of both harmony (i.e. chords) and melody (i.e. playing single notes).

JIMMY PAGE
The legendary Jimmy Page, who filled Eric Clapton's (later Jeff Beck's) spot in The Yardbirds, founded perhaps the super-est of all supergroups, Led Zepellin, in 1968. Famous for occasional playing with a violin bow, and for his heavily overdriven amplified electric sound, Page is the archetype for generations of rock guitarists.

GOAL: *TO AUDITION A COUPLE OF DIFFERENT METHODS FOR SOUNDING THE STRINGS ON YOUR GUITAR.
TO PLAY YOUR FIRST ARPEGGIATED CHORD – SOUNDING A CHORD ONE STRING AT A TIME – MEANING 'HARP-LIKE'.*

In the last Chapter we began looking at the idea of using a plectrum or pick to play single melody notes. Naturally, you can use a pick to play chords, too.

You may have already experimented a little with this yourself, in fact. In general, acoustic guitarists are split into two main groups when it comes to sounding the strings with the right hand: one group prefer using picks while the other use their fingers.

NB: There are a couple of hybrid right-hand styles – players who use thumb picks (a plectrum-like device that clips onto the thumb leaving the fingers free) or finger picks (very similar to thumb picks except that they clip onto the fingers) for instance – but the two main groups divide themselves into using either plastic or good, honest flesh.

There are a whole lot of reasons why players eventually end up going for one or the other but the principal reason is down to tone. The fact is that if you strike the strings of your guitar with anything made from plastic it's going to sound different than it would do if it's strummed with the fingers.

If we refine the exact manner in which the strings are struck (with either plastic or flesh) still further, more subtle nuances of tone or timbre – as it's known in music – become available.

WORKOUT 1

Most of this, of course, awaits you in the future.
Right now we're more concerned with chord shapes and
the scale I introduced you to in the last Chapter, but I
thought it would be a good idea to show you a couple
of things that will serve to illustrate the differences
in sound and texture between pick and fingers.
Take a look at the example below:

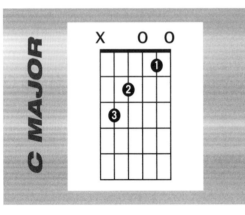

This is a chord we haven't met before called C major.
To begin with, work from the chord box above and go
through the usual checklist where positioning the fingers
is concerned. You might find that it's a bit of a stretch
for the third left-hand finger, but remember that this is
an area where nature needs a nudge so the feeling that
your hand is going to split in half will soon go away.

WORKOUT 2

Once you're familiar with the shape and can get a good
clean note out of each of the strings, take a look at the
next example.

Now don't panic, all we have here is the same C major
chord we looked at previously but this time it's in
tablature and played one string at a time.

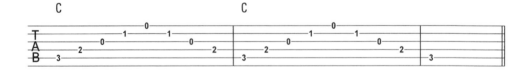

Hold down the chord shape as shown in the DVD and play the strings one at a time with a pick.

As with everything, it's going to feel strange at first, and probably sound a little strange, too, but you've got the DVD as a reference point so that you can hear what it should sound like.

Next, try plucking each of the strings in the exercise with your finger. Any finger will do at this point, we'll look at the fancy stuff later.

Try to hear the difference in tone: the pick should make things sound more solid and probably louder, too, whereas your finger will give a slightly quieter and generally more subtle sound.

Playing the different strings of a chord, one after the other like this, is known as playing *arpeggios*. These crop up a great deal in instrumental music of all kinds.

PERFORMANCE PIECE

Now we are going to play this chord over a backing track so you can hear what it sounds like when used as an accompaniment idea.

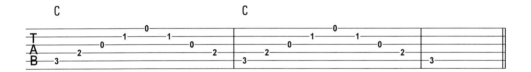

SUMMARY

Now you have experienced the basic difference between fingerstyle – as playing with the fingers is called – and using a plectrum. Like I say, you don't have to make any decisions as to which you prefer now, but it's never too early to point out the differences between pick and finger playing.

PLAYING MELODY

It is time to amass everything we've looked at into a cohesive whole and play some melody. So, without any further ado, we'll get straight down to it.

To an acoustic player, learning a song usually means getting together the bare essentials needed to accompany a singer, but occasionally we get the chance to play the melody, too. So we're going to take a look at how this might come about in a simple arrangement I've put together specially.

First of all, a little revision. Remember that chord sequence from a couple of Chapters back? How could you forget? You've been practising it every day, haven't you? Just for reference, here it is again:

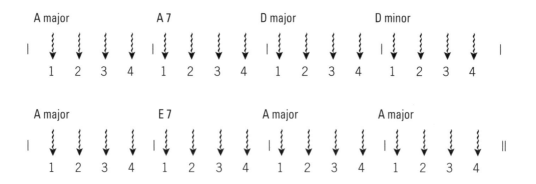

Now look at this:

WORKOUT 1

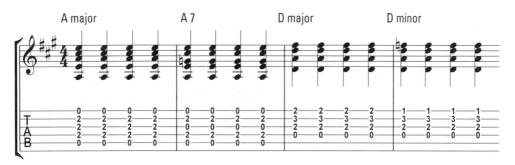

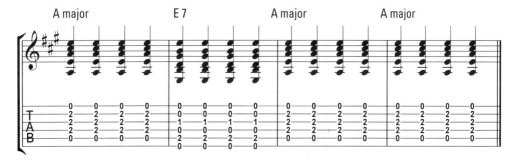

Looks a little serious doesn't it? After all, it's proper-looking music. But fear not, because all this represents is the chord exercise you've been playing all along in the form of musical notation. This is how guitar music looks when you buy it from a shop in book form and something that you'll become very familiar with in the future.

So why have I gone to all the trouble of writing out something you already know? The answer is that you're not going to play this part any more, not in this Chapter anyway. You're going to play a melody over the top.

WORKOUT 2

This melody, in fact:

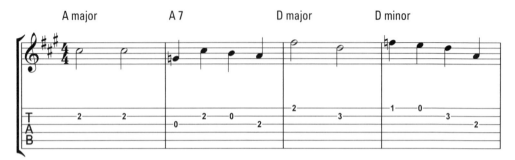

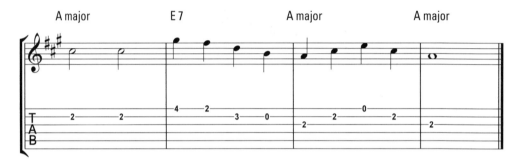

This probably strikes you as being a little ambitious, seeing as we're only a third of the way through the book. But everything looks far more complicated than it really is when it's written out in musical notation so you can be sure that your melody part is actually just demanding enough to keep you on your toes, but definitely not so hard it will keep you awake at night.

I hope you remembered to count your way through the chord exercise when you were practising it back in Chapter 5, because that basic training will stand you in good stead here.

To begin with, work your way through the melody part one bar at a time, and listen hard to the audio file to make sure that what you are playing matches my version exactly. This is a good practice to adopt when learning any piece of music. Look at it in bite-sized chunks only and don't be tempted to rush ahead as this leads to mistakes and poor memory retention.

SUMMARY

You are free to play the melody part using either a pick or your fingers (or thumb) but a pick would be my own personal recommendation as the notes will definitely sound louder and cleaner this way around.

Once you have mastered the melody part to the extent that you can play it through with no mistakes, have a go at playing it over the backing track. It's a very good idea to continually refer to the 'whole' version on the disc as this will give you a good idea what you're aiming to achieve. Whatever you do, don't become impatient and frustrated with the song if things begin to fall apart. It happens to everyone. Even established pros have to learn new pieces and usually end up making several goofs before they arrive at a perfect performance.

PERFORMANCE PIECE

Now let's put it all together. Here's the complete piece
for you to work through with the backing track.

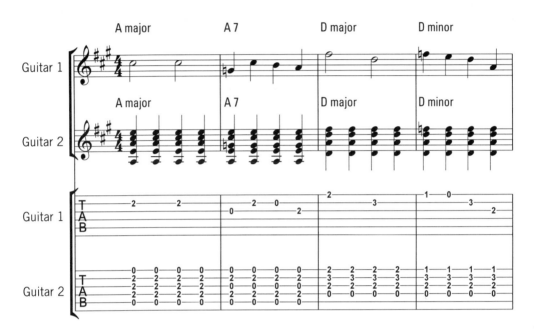

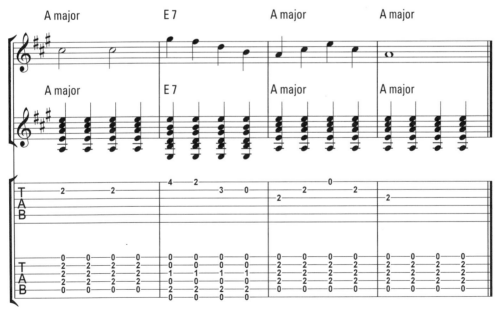

GOAL: TO EXPAND OUR CHORD VOCABULARY, AND TO LEARN THE CORRECT GUITARISTS' CHORD TERMINOLOGY.

CHORD VOCABULARY

The next step on your path towards becoming an all-round acoustic player is to reinforce your knowledge of chords: something which we'll be turning our attention towards in a moment. However, for now we just want to make sure that your practice routine is working efficiently.

You should be putting aside half an hour or so every day to run through the things we are learning. We've covered quite a lot of ground so far and it all needs reviewing regularly to make sure that it stays in your memory. We've been careful to make sure that all the Chapters are progressive, but also that they don't conflict too much with one another or pay too much attention to a single area for too long. The last Chapter focused on melody and now it's time to return to chords.

Learning chords is essentially increasing your vocabulary. Too many players try to learn inappropriate chords too soon. These are things they won't need either for a long time or ever, in fact. What we're teaching you here is forming part of your core curriculum as a player and you'll be able to play a great many songs with just these chords alone. So eyes, down, let's get some more shapes under those fingers.

WORKOUT 1

First of all, here is G major:

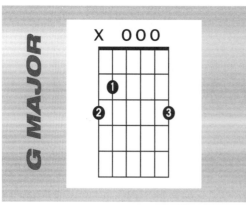

The tricky part here is the stretch between fingers one, two and three. Once again, remember that it might feel difficult now, but there are muscles to condition, reflexes to sharpen and nothing will do the job quicker than practice.

WORKOUT 2

Next in line we have G7:

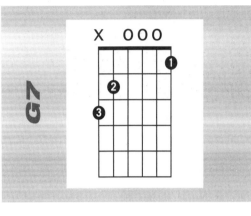

It is another stretchy chord (which is why I've left it this long to introduce it into your repertoire). Be patient and persevere: it will get easier.

WORKOUT 3

Let's look at C7 now:

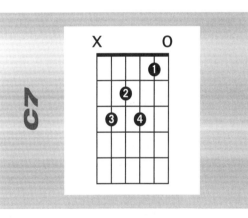

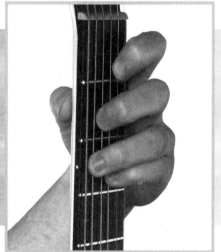

Now it's time for the weakest member of the left hand artillery to join the action. Needless to say, your little finger is going to be a little sluggish and slow to come on line, but give it a chance, as it's probably had an easy life so far. Remember to sound each string and only let it through quality control if it's free from buzzes and completely mute-free.

WORKOUT 4

Here's another chord that uses all four fingers of the left hand. B7:

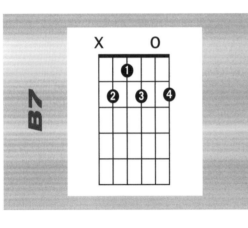

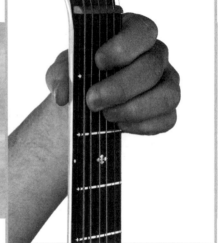

An added handicap here is the fact that all the fingers are now operating in quite a narrow space on the fretboard so you'll probably have to let them 'settle in' for a while before everything sounds clean.

WORKOUT 5

Now, remember that I said that there are basically 36 chords to learn before you get to the more exotic variations later on? Well, if your maths is at least as good as mine, you'll have noticed that we're still quite a few short. This is because the rest of the chord shapes tend to be a little more difficult. As an example, let's look at the nemesis of many a guitar student, namely the F chord:

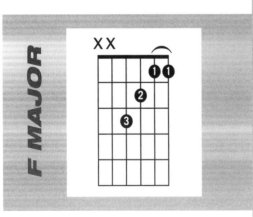

At first glance, it looks innocent enough, but check out the fingering; finger one is expected to hold down two notes instead of the one it's been used to... so what's going on? Oddly enough, asking one finger to hold down several notes at once is really common in guitar playing. There's even a word for it; it's known as a *barre* (pronounced 'bar' but spelt differently to confuse non-guitarists). It's something we can't get by without learning and everyone finds it nearly impossible to begin with. Take a good look at the recommendations for dealing with this difficult customer on the DVD. You will find it easy in the end.

PERFORMANCE PIECE

Finally, for this Chapter, here is a chord sequence to practise some of your new chord collection. Don't panic, I've not included an F major!

Chord terminology:

Up till now, we've written out the chord names in full, but conventional guitar notation uses a simple abbreviation, so let's follow suit. Major chords do without the word 'major', simply stating the note on which the chord begins. Therefore, C major is generally written as C. For minor chords, a simple 'm' will suffice, so A minor is more usually written as Am. Check out the new system below, as this is how we'll be referring to chords from now on.

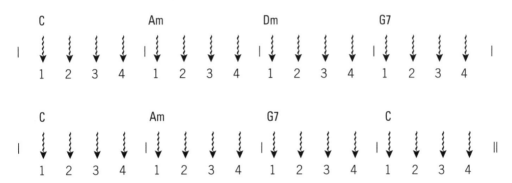

SUMMARY

So now you should have some idea about how building a chord vocabulary can expand your facilities as a guitar player, and you've an idea about how to go about the task, too. You have learnt a few new chords – including the dreaded F – and there is a new piece to learn. Sounds like a good day at the office to me!

GOAL: *TO INTRODUCE NEW TIME SIGNATURES.*

THE RHYTHM BUSINESS

Up until now, you've been playing chord sequences 'four to the bar', although I hope you've experimented a little with using the upstrokes we looked at back in Chapter 2. We have looked a little at arpeggios, too. The fact is that both these devices are useful in making a right-hand strumming pattern more interesting and both are something the professional acoustic players use all the time.

If we use straight 'fours' or 'eighths' to accompany every song we play, everything is going to sound very military and precise, so the thing to do is to learn to mix things up a little. Of course, we've still got to pay very strict attention to the basic *pulse* of the music. We mustn't ever lose track of the fundamental beat of the music we're playing otherwise everything will turn into an anarchic mess. So, what sort of measures can we take to make sure that the rhythm is still strong, but the role of the right hand never becomes boring?

WORKOUT 1

To begin with, let's take a closer look at the business of rhythm itself. We've seen how music usually has four beats to the bar, like this:

So far, we have accented the four beats with a downstroke with the fingers or pick. Sometimes, though, you might find that the music you're playing has a pulse of three beats to the bar, as in a waltz, for instance.

Sometimes, you might even find two beats per bar:

This kind of thing is often found in marches. Two feet, with one beat per foot: *left, right, left, right…*

The fact is that music can have almost any number of beats per bar, but before you have a panic attack I assure you that you'll be dealing with the timings listed above most of the time.

WORKOUT 2

Now, I don't intend to go too far into the maths of music, but in order to give the right hand something more interesting to do we're going to have to take a brief look at how we can split a single beat up a bit a little more.

So far, we have downstrokes, giving us a four-to-the-bar rhythm:

And we've looked at *eighths*, employing upstrokes and downstrokes:

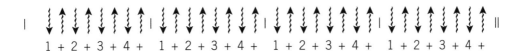

WORKOUT 3

There is a smaller option available to us, where we split each beat into four parts, giving us *sixteenths*: a combination down-up-down-up picking pattern:

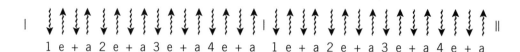

1 e + a 2 e + a 3 e + a 4 e + a   1 e + a 2 e + a 3 e + a 4 e + a

If you're wondering what the 'e + a' is all about, it's a way of counting sixteenths. All is made clear on the DVD.

Now we have three different things that the right hand can do to make an accompaniment more interesting, but there is a fourth: silence. You don't have to play on every beat of the bar, in fact, few players do, so 'missing out' beats is another way of adding interest.

The question of mixing everything up to make a more absorbing rhythmic pattern can be reduced to maths, like this:

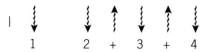 

1   2 + 3 + 4   1 e + a 2 + 3 + 4

PERFORMANCE PIECE

Go back through some of the chord sequences we have looked at and randomise your right-hand strumming pattern. See what happens... for instance, you could try this one:

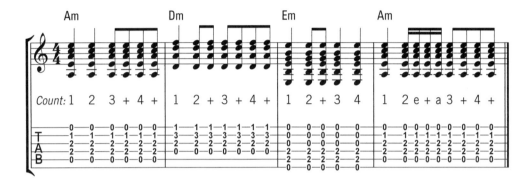

I've given you a couple of ideas, and there are more to look at on the DVD. The only thing you've got to be careful about is to make sure that each bar 'adds up' to four. In other words, make sure the maths is right. You'll find that some patterns work better than others, but in any case doing exercises like this one is a good workout for the right hand.

SUMMARY

So now you should be aware that there is more that can be done with the right hand than just simple four-to-the-bar strumming. It really is only with experimentation that players find their way in this respect so I would urge you to do just that: listen to what's happening on acoustic guitar in the music you enjoy and try to work it out and copy it.

GOAL: INSTEAD OF LOOKING AT PURE RHYTHMIC STRUMMING, WE ARE GOING TO LOOK AT THE BARE BONES OF FINGERSTYLE.

At present, you've got quite a lot of data to process: chords to learn, rhythm patterns to explore and even some melody studies to look through. All of this ought to form your essential 'work in progress', although I appreciate that it might be impossible to assign time to work through everything during a single practice session. As long as you continue to review everything we've studied together so far regularly, your playing will continue on track.

NB: I've mentioned before that a lot of players use their fingers instead of a plectrum to strike or pluck the strings and many of them have developed this facility to quite a high degree. Obviously a state of considerable dexterity with the right-hand fingers doesn't come cheap, but luckily the only real cost is that of a lot of time dedicated to practice.

Whatever course you decide to take in the pick or fingers debate, it's a good idea to have a look at the foundation skills necessary for fingerstyle in order to help you make up your mind which is right for you.

LEONARD COHEN
Canadian singer-sonwriter and poet Leonard Cohen is best-known as a guitarist for his simple, sometimes sparse strumming and picking accompaniments, the perfect foil for his often complex and intense vocal lines.

WORKOUT 1

To begin with, we are going to make it as easy as possible and practise some basic finger skills on open strings. As there's nothing for your left hand to do, it will give you more opportunity to concentrate on the right alone. Look at the music example below:

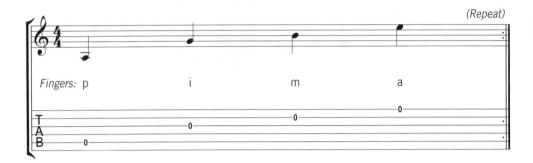

In order to play this exercise, you need to place your thumb on the bass A string and your index, middle and ring fingers on the top three strings:

Index: G string
Middle: B string
Ring: top E string

If there is any doubt, take a look at the DVD to make sure that you're on the right track.

It is unlikely that you'll have long fingernails on your right hand, so we're going to have to use good honest flesh instead to sound the strings. (A lot of fingerstyle players grow their right-hand nails, often resorting to reinforcing them with acrylic or some kind of industrial strength nail varnish to ward off wear and tear from the metal strings.)

Sound each of the strings carefully and try to make as little movement as possible with the hand itself, as this is a job for the fingers alone.

WORKOUT 2

Next, we will add a few variations to the fingerstyle
pattern to mix things up a little.

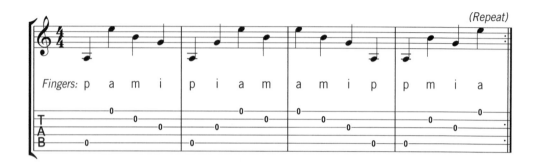

You will need to work through the exercise carefully to
make sure that you've got it spot on before proceeding
any further. Check with my version to make sure you're
on track.

WORKOUT 3

You're probably getting tired of hearing those open
strings all the time so let's throw in a couple of chord
shapes and bring the left hand back into play.

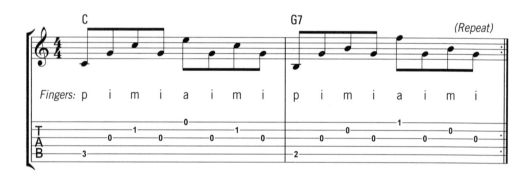

PERFORMANCE PIECE

Here you have fingerstyle patterns for three chords and now we're going to string them together to make a song accompaniment.

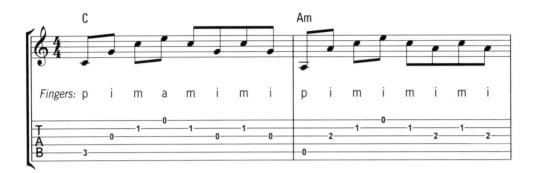

SUMMARY

This is a good example of what you can do with your fingers, as opposed to strumming with a pick. As I said earlier, it's a good idea to familiarise yourself with these rudiments as they can prove to be very effective as a contrast to pick work. Ideally, you want to be as versatile as possible and cover as broad a base as you can in these early stages. The time to settle on a style and specialise is still in the future.

GOAL: *TO INTRODUCE THE BARRE AND CONSOLIDATE THE CHORDS STUDIED UP TILL NOW.*

BARRE CHORDS

Let's return to the issue of chord vocabulary. As we saw a few Chapters back, we have looked at less than half of the essential '36 pack' of chords and I told you that this was because the rest of them were a little more difficult. In truth, I think that you're better off learning a new technique that will open up the subject of learning chords once and for all: it's called the full barre.

Remember when we looked at the F major chord where it's necessary to hold down two notes with a single finger? You doubtless found it very difficult to begin with, but time and effort will pay off in the end, even if your 'F' still isn't ringing loud and clear quite yet. As I've said before, we've all been there before and we've all come through the 'F barrier' so perseverance is very much the name of the game here.

Before we get on with looking at a full barre, let's review the 15 chords you already know – it's handy to have them all in one place because it will save you turning back pages to check up on them if your memory is still a bit rusty.

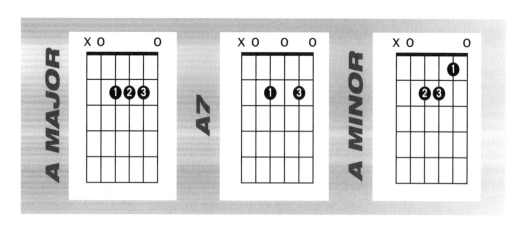

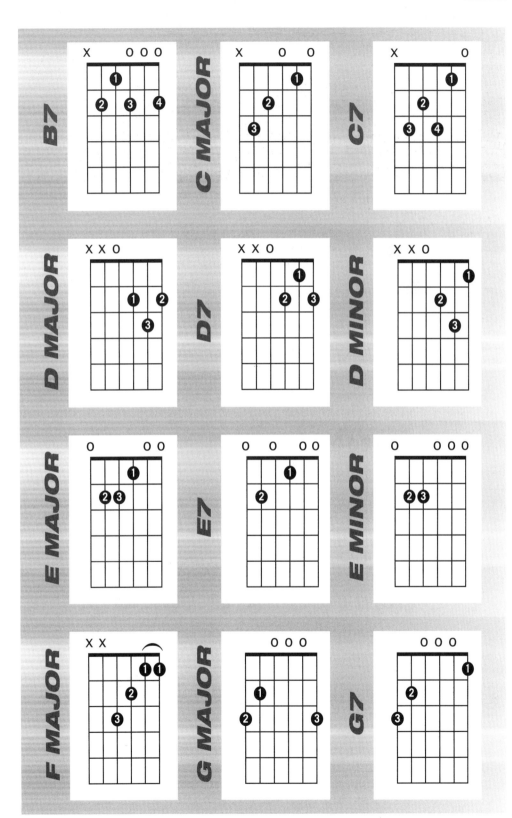

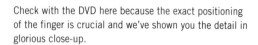

WORKOUT 1

The next thing to try is to lay your left-hand index finger across all of the strings, like this:

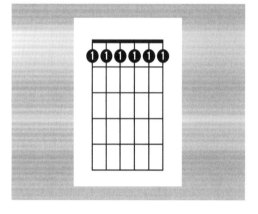

WORKOUT 2

Once again, here is your basic barre:

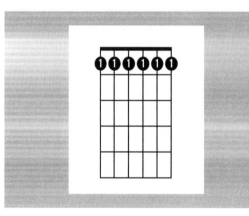

If you placed two fingers here, you would have a shape that looks very similar to the first chord we learned together:

Check with the DVD here because the exact positioning of the finger is crucial and we've shown you the detail in glorious close-up.

What you need to do now is sound each of the guitar strings individually and make sure that you have a clear note out of every one. Very few people manage to pull this off first time so don't despair if your initial attempt only gives you two or three notes out of six. Keep trying.

You'll find, too, that the muscle between your left-hand thumb and index finger is very weak or, at least, not quite up to the task of holding down all six strings on a guitar for very long. After all, it wasn't exactly in the design brief for the hand so we mustn't complain. Time will strengthen up the muscles and you won't even have to think about playing barres soon enough.

Now I'm quite prepared to believe that you've literally got your hands full with the full barre, but I thought I'd give you a glimpse of the future to illustrate how useful the system of barre chords is going to be to you.

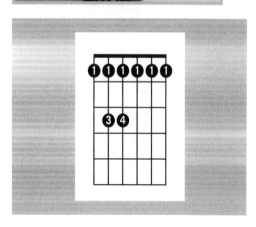

If you've just tried to play the chord in the exercise above and yelped in pain while doing so, fear not, it will take you a few more weeks before this sort of thing even begins to feel natural. The point is, this chord is self-contained and moveable, which means that you can play it anywhere on the neck and get different minor chords just by moving it around. So, if there are 12 frets, 12 notes in the chromatic scale and 12 places to play this chord, you've learned 12 chords from one shape.

It will take a while for the full impact of what barre chords can mean to you to sink in, and we have demonstrated the idea more fully on the DVD. But if learning to play barre chords means that you learn 12 chords at once, it's got to be worth all the hours of work training the hand to do it, hasn't it?

WORKOUT 3
And it doesn't end there. Take a look here for future reference:

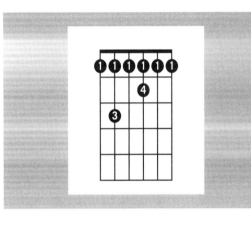

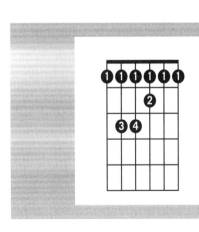

These chords come from a basic barre and will save you a lot of time learning those remaining shapes from our 36 (and many more besides).

PERFORMANCE PIECE

So for this Chapter, your assignment is a simple one: lay the index finger across the neck and get six clearly ringing notes in various places on the neck, like this:

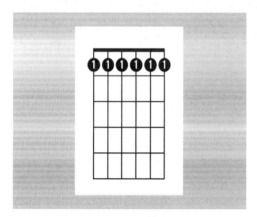

It might not sound terribly musical, and no backing track is going to glamorise it for you, it's just down to some hard graft for the left hand.

SUMMARY

Every guitar player relies on barre chords. They are probably the most important chords you'll ever learn, but I've found that guitarists often come to them too late because they find them difficult.
I tend to introduce them to my students as early as possible in order that the necessary muscles begin to develop in good time.

GOAL: TO BE ABLE TO CHANGE THE KEY OF ANY SONG INSTANTLY, WITHOUT THE ENCUMBRANCE OF LEARNING THE MUSIC THEORY IN ORDER TO BE ABLE TO DO SO.

USING A CAPO

Of course there is another way of expanding the repertoire of chords you've already learned. It's more immediate and less bothersome than learning barre chords – although I still strongly advise you to take that particular course – but it does rely on you buying another bit of gear. Fear not, it's probably something you would end up buying in any case, it's just a question of it being now rather than later.

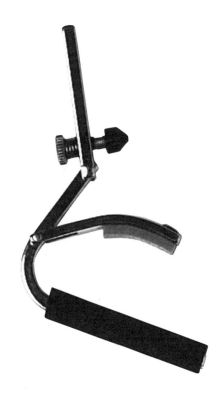

To begin with, let me tell you about a situation that crops up all the time when you either work with a singer, or want to sing some songs and accompany yourself on the guitar.

First of all you get hold of the music, learn the chords and make the whole thing playable. Next, you either arrange to meet up with someone who sings or you have a go yourself. Around 60 per cent of the time everything is fine and you end up with a very respectable performance of whatever it is you wanted to learn. But sometimes you find that the song you've learned just isn't right for your voice at all. It might be that you have to affect a shrieking falsetto or a floor-shaking bass vocal register to get the melody to work, and usually something has to give.

That something can mean a lot of musical mental arithmetic in that one way around the situation is to *transpose* the song into another key. Now you don't need me to tell you that transposing is strictly for the more advanced music students and certainly not for someone who is just over half the way through their first 24 lessons. It means learning the song again with all new chords and re-covering an awful lot of ground while you learn it. But this is where a wonderful little gizmo called a 'capo' comes in.

As you'll see on the DVD, a capo is a little mechanical device that sits on the guitar neck and clamps all the strings down at a selected point on the fretboard. It's sort of like an automatic barre machine, except that you can't move it during a song and you've still got all your fingers free to form chords.

WORKOUT 1

Let's look at a chord arrangement from earlier on in the
book. Remember this one?

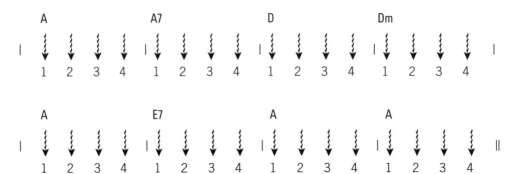

So far, you've just been playing this arrangement down
at the nut, but if we put a capo on the guitar at the third
fret, it alters all the chord names to these:

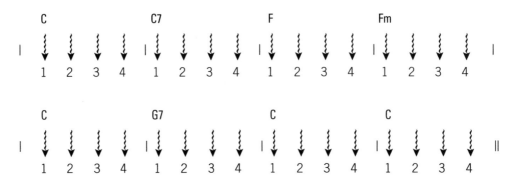

WORKOUT 2

Put the capo on the sixth fret and you have this:

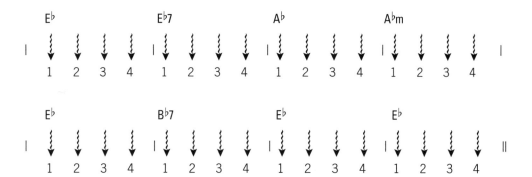

In other words, you would end up playing a whole lot of chords you don't actually know, but the actual chord shapes would all be the same as before.

There are two ways in which this is important to us: one immediate way and another that will come into play much later on.

To begin with, you will be able to get around the 'vocal range' problem I mentioned earlier with consummate ease; it literally won't be a problem. That's the immediate value. Later on, as your general savvy with chords, and so on improves and deepens, you'll be able to be a little more strategic in the way you use a capo. In other words, you'll know that placing it at the sixth fret will give you those precise chords and that using a capo makes them so much easier to play.

PERFORMANCE PIECE

SUMMARY

So your assignment for this Chapter is to practise some of the pieces we've looked at but now employing a capo at various points on the neck to hear the difference it makes. The actual music science may be beyond you at present, but having this sort of facility at your disposal at this stage in your development literally quadruples your range as an accompanist.

Here are a couple of pieces to try:

At the risk of repeating myself, I believe that the purchase of a capo at this stage will do wonders for your playing. If, for instance, you're bored stiff with hearing yourself practise the same old exercises, try using your capo to make them sound fresh. The more you use it, the more adaptable you will become as a player. Go for it!

Open position

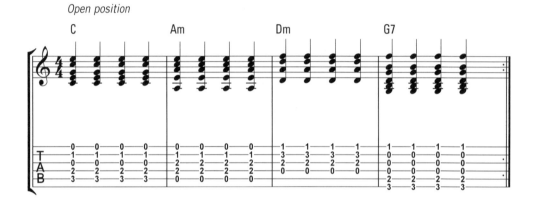

Capo on third fret

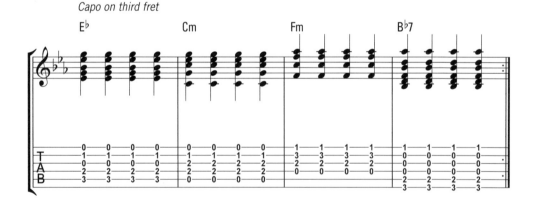

GOAL: TO UNDERSTAND THE NATURE AND APPLICATION OF SCALES.

MORE SCALES

I realise that you've probably got your hands full with all the various things we've been looking at. I'm trying to keep each individual lesson as varied as possible so that you don't have too much of the same thing to practise at any one time. I'm also trying to give you as broad a base as possible, trying to cover a lot of ground so that you are prepared for taking your playing on further after you have finished this course.

We've looked extensively at chords and strumming techniques – even a little bit of fingerstyle – but now it's time to return to the question of melody playing and take a further look at the world of scales.

I know that it's traditional for all students of guitar to think that scales are boring, and I'd be the first one to agree with you, believe it or not. But they are important: all melodies come from scales so they represent the raw materials from which all your adventures with single-string playing are formed. Learning to get your fingers around individual notes and making sure that both hands know their individual roles where melody is concerned is vital so let's take another few steps together.

WORKOUT 1

Take a look at this example:

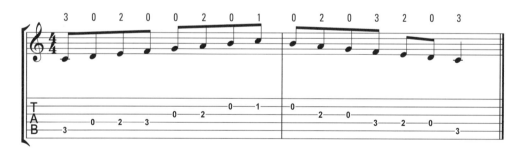

This is a C major scale down at the nut. If you are going to play it with a plectrum, make sure you use alternate picking as shown in the DVD. By the way, notice that the left-hand fingering is now shown above the notes.

WORKOUT 2

Next, we will look at an E major scale:

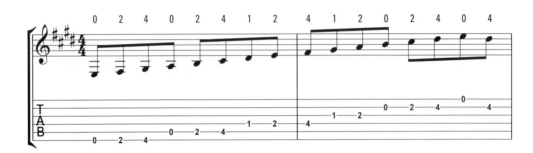

This is a slightly longer scale as it covers all six strings. If you take it slowly – and keep checking your picking – all should be well.

Remember to look at the left-hand fingering, too. It's not a good idea to do too much moving around with the left hand: it's better to let the fingers find the notes with the absolute minimum movement possible. The more economic you are here, the more fluent your scale playing will sound. So even if your left-hand little finger won't do a thing you want it to at first, be patient and it will begin to obey orders with practice.

WORKOUT 3

Okay: two more scales and we're done for this Chapter.
Here is the first:

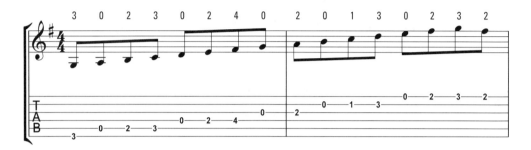

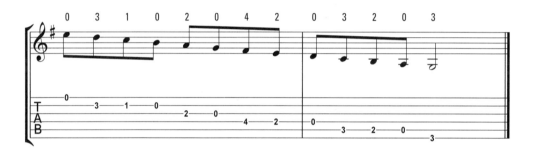

This is a G major scale. The rules are the same as
before: keep an eye on both hands at all times; minimise
the movement in the left hand; and make those fingers
do all the running around.

WORKOUT 4

Here is our final scale:

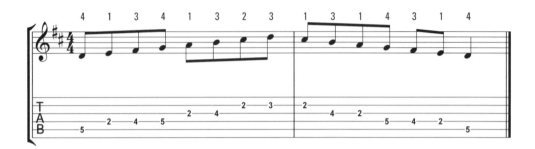

It's a D major scale. Take thing slowly and make sure you get a good clear note out of every fret. Notice especially that certain notes that you've previously played on open strings are now being fingered on the 4th and 5th frets. You'll need to move the whole left hand up the neck a little to adjust for this new position. If things start sounding muted or buzzy, change your left-hand position until things become clear again.

B. B. KING
B. B. King is one of the most influential and well-respected guitarists of all time. Often called 'The King of Blues', his wailing lead lines are instantly recognisable. In common with many electric blues guitarists, his style can easily be traced to the acoustic heroes of the early Southern blues such as Leadbelly and Robert Johnson.

PERFORMANCE PIECE

Just to give you some idea of how musical a scale can be, I've provided a backing track for you to practise the C scale over. See if you can make it sound the same as my example on the audio track.

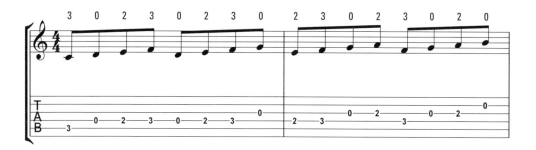

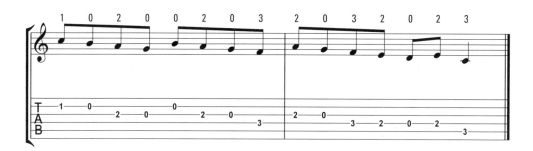

SUMMARY

Scales thread themselves through music like letters through a stick of rock, so learning them is essential for any instrumentalist. Now that you have made some initial steps in learning and playing scales, your fingers' agility and, more importantly, your sense of music will be greatly enhanced.

GOAL: TO EXPLORE A 12-BAR BLUES CHORD PROGRESSION AND LEARN TO RIFF ON IT.

PLAYING THE BLUES

Sometimes when you are called upon to accompany a song, you won't necessarily be expected to play chords.
Different styles of music have their own characteristics in this respect, and probably the most obvious one to look at is the blues.

You don't have to be a blues devotee to make use of the information in this Chapter. This basic style of accompaniment can be found in plenty of rock and roll and even country styles. What's more, it is something you will instantly recognise and bags of fun to play, too.

Before we look at the accompaniment figure, I'll let you know a couple of things about the blues. As a form of music, the blues is pretty much unique in that it doesn't have a chorus. Most songs are written to a basic formula that goes something like this:

Verse, verse, chorus, verse...

If you listen to two or three songs at random you can bet that they'll fall into this formula, but not in the case of the blues. In this particular idiom, there is no chorus as such, just 12 bars of music repeated over and over again. For this reason, you'll often hear guitarists refer to something called a *12-bar blues* and that's what they mean.

The other thing you need to know – and I guarantee you'll like this – is that the average blues has only three chords in it.

WORKOUT 1

Let's look at a basic 12-bar blues. First of all, we'll look at the basic chords involved:

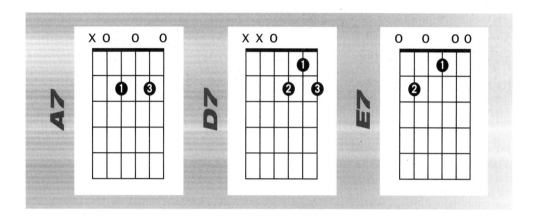

And now, here's the chord chart. This chart is slightly different to the ones we've seen so far as the name of the chord is on the first beat in the bar and the rest of the beats are signified by *slashes*, like this:

| A7 / / / |A7 / / / |A7 / / / |A7 / / / |

| D7 / / / |D7 / / / |A7 / / / |A7 / / / |

| E7 / / / |D7 / / / |A7 / / / |A7 / / / ‖

You would still count through the chart '1 2 3 4' as before, but this way is neater and more like the kind of charts you'll see in books and so on.

To begin with, it might be a good idea to work through the chart playing the chords, just to familiarise yourself with the basic feel and shape of the thing.

WORKOUT 2

Next, we'll look at a little figure that you can play instead of the chords:

You would play this where the chord chart calls for an A7. Listen carefully to my recorded version to make sure you are playing it right before moving on.

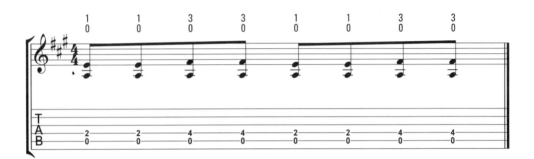

WORKOUT 3

Next, here's the figure you will play instead of the D7. As you can see, it's exactly the same as the one we played for A7, it's just on a different pair of strings.

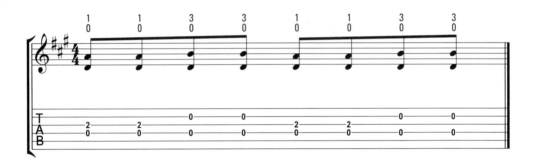

WORKOUT 4

Lastly, here's the E7 version:

If you check the chart, you will see that you only have to play this one once and it's quite a quick change between this, the A7 and D7. In other words, you are going to have to take some time mastering changing between all three figures – literally hopping over the strings with your fingers – before you can expect everything to start flowing smoothly. If you watch the DVD at this point, you can see this sequence being played and pick up some recommendations for making the movements in between as economical as possible.

PERFORMANCE PIECE

Finally, here is the whole 12-bar blues written out in tab to make it easier for you to follow. Take things slowly at first and don't even dream about speeding up until all those changes are as smooth as silk.

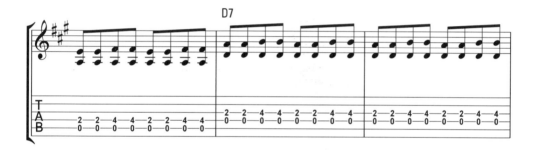

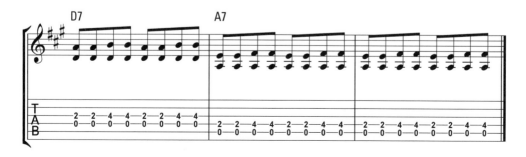

SUMMARY

Blues is like a common language in music. It connects the various instruments together because it's guaranteed that everyone comes across it fairly early on in their studies.
In fact, it's often the first thing musicians learn to play together, such is its appeal.
So equipping yourself with the basics of blues accompaniment is another step towards being an acoustic guitar all-rounder.

ROBERT JOHNSON
Blues guitar master Johnson's 40-odd acoustic recordings are some of the best and most reliable existing documents of early Delta Blues. His distinctive vocal style, part-growl and part-whine, interweave perfectly with his deft finger-work. An absolute must for acoustic aficionados.

GOAL: TO EXPLORE STRUMMING VARIATIONS FOR EFFECTIVE ACCOMPANIMENT.

PLAYING THE CHANGES

In this Chapter, we are going to look at a whole song: a complete chord arrangement for you to play over a backing track. I won't use any controversial chord shapes that will trip you up, as we'll stick to fairly easy elements here. But I'm trusting that your practice routine is chock full with 'work in progress' as far as the more demanding chords, accompaniment patterns and scales are concerned.

The only thing that will get the more awkward material fully up and running is good old practice, so you have to put the work in, even if those hands are still misbehaving and occasionally not doing what they're told.

This song will have a contemporary feel to it. I've aimed it so that it sounds very similar to the sort of thing you would hear in the charts from any of the new acoustic singer-songwriter generation.

WORKOUT 1

To begin with, here's a chart showing all of the chords used in the song:

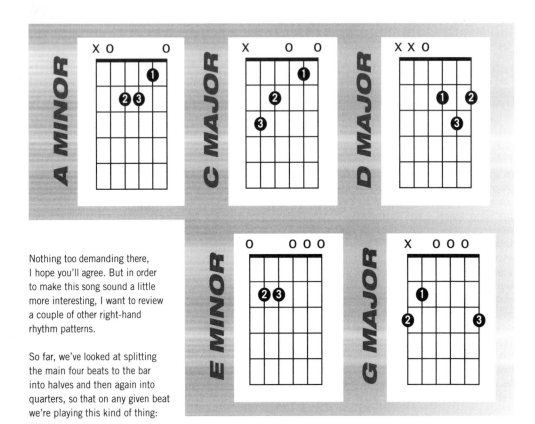

Nothing too demanding there, I hope you'll agree. But in order to make this song sound a little more interesting, I want to review a couple of other right-hand rhythm patterns.

So far, we've looked at splitting the main four beats to the bar into halves and then again into quarters, so that on any given beat we're playing this kind of thing:

Downstrokes:

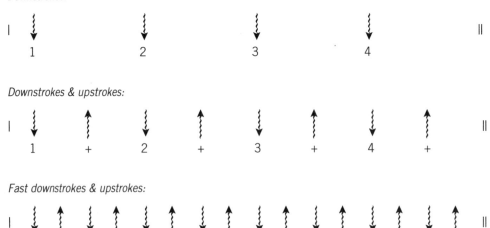

Downstrokes & upstrokes:

Fast downstrokes & upstrokes:

All well and good, but even this is going to start sounding tiresome before too long if it's repeated over and over again, military style. We need even more variation thrown in there to keep everything sounding fresh. So, rather than putting any more movement into the bar, let's try leaving things out.

WORKOUT 2

Sometimes, it's enough to play a chord on the first beat and hold it for the whole bar, like this:

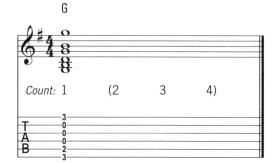

Sometimes it sounds good to play on beats one and three, like this:

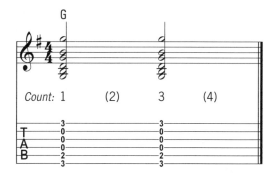

An effective rhythmic device is to hold a chord over a beat, in order to make things sound a little 'off centre'.

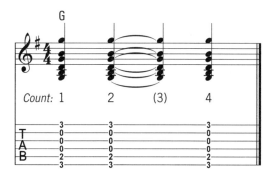

You will need to watch the DVD and listen to the audio carefully to hear what I mean about a chord being 'held over' a beat, but I think you'll agree that it certainly breaks things up nicely and I bet you've heard it often in the past.

PERFORMANCE PIECE

On to our song then. Here's the chord arrangement:

| G / / / |Em / / / | C / / / | D / / / |

| G / / / |Em / / / | C / / / | D / / / |

| Em / / / |Am / / / |Em / / / | D / / / |

| G / / / |Em / / / | C / / / | D / / / ‖

The chord arrangement repeats but at the end, play

| G / / / ‖

SUMMARY

This Chapter begins to assemble all the skills you'll need at your disposal when you begin to work through the songs you want to learn. By implementing a system like the one I've illustrated here, you should find that navigating your way through more challenging material later on is made simpler.

And here are a few suggestions for rhythm in tab. Watch the DVD for details.

Once you're sure that your version of the accompaniment is absolutely cast iron, play it along with the backing track for the full effect.

(Play through twice)

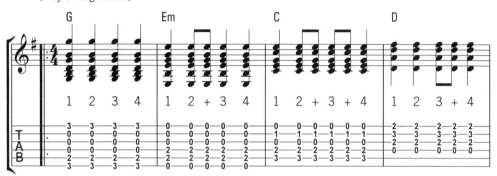

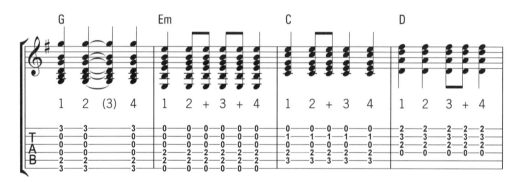

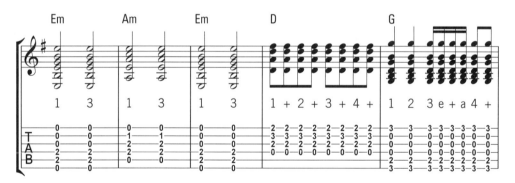

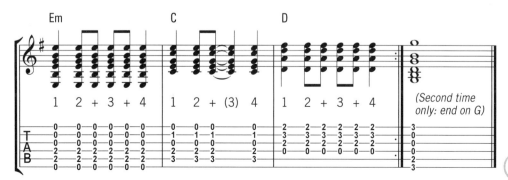

83

GOAL: WE ARE GOING TO BEGIN TO MAKE FULL USE OF BARRE CHORDS BY LEARNING SOME SHAPES THAT COVER THE THREE BASIC CHORD FAMILIES: MAJOR, MINOR AND DOMINANT SEVENTHS.
THE NEXT STEP IN THIS RESPECT IS FOR THE REMAINING THREE FINGERS ON THAT HAND TO LEARN A FEW SHAPES AND FILL IN THE BLANKS IN YOUR CHORD REPERTOIRE AT THE SAME TIME.

BARRE CHORDS II

In this Chapter we are returning to the subject of barre chords. Hopefully you have been practising holding down all six strings with your left-hand index finger the way I showed you back in Chapter 12 and it's now beginning to feel easier.

WORKOUT 1

First of all, let's look at two major barre chord shapes. The first one looks like an E major shape. Notice also that the barre is depicted by a curved line joining the limits of the barre, but that the finger 'dots' are only shown for the strings on which the barre sounds (compare to the diagrams in Chapter 12 which showed the barre on every string, regardless of whether other fingers were also placed on that string). In the example below the barre is across all six strings:

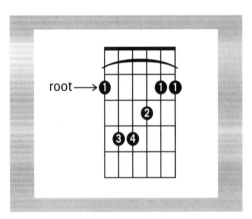

Don't worry if it feels absolutely impossible and sounds completely wonky the first time you try it: that's where practice comes in. It's important to use the correct fingering and run through the checklist of things to watch out for as shown on the DVD.

WORKOUT 2

The next shape is another major barre chord. This one looks very similar to an A major chord.

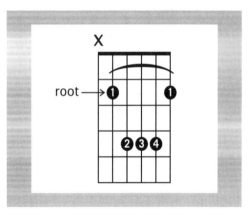

This is one of two fingerings available for this chord. The one above is actually easier to begin with, but a lot of players end up using this alternative:

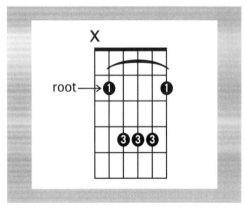

I know what you're going to say: how on earth do I get my third finger to hold down three strings at once? The fact is that nature still has a few party tricks to pull off with the joints of your fingers – in time they will become far more supple, or 'bendy' – and the third finger will be able to hold down these three strings with no trouble at all. However, for now it is probably better that you try the first fingering and wait for nature to work its magic a little later on.

WORKOUT 3

All the barres we will be looking at now are variations on the two shapes above. For instance, take a look at the two minor shapes below:

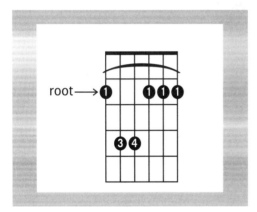

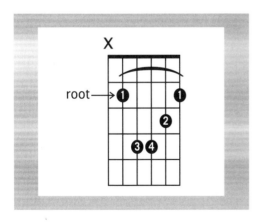

The first one looks like E minor, the second one A minor, so you already 'know' the shapes. It's just the new fingerings and the mediaeval torture of holding down the barre itself that you have to come to terms with.

WORKOUT 4

The next two shapes are both sevenths. Once again, they're both dead ringers for shapes you already know.

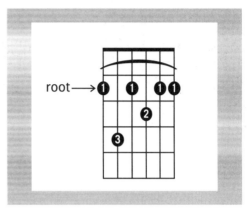

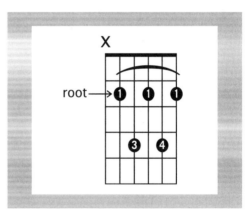

The upper one looks like E7 and the lower one is a direct descendent of A7. As before, pay attention to the fingerings. Above everything else, have patience as no one ever gets these chords under their fingers on the first attempt.

PERFORMANCE PIECE

It would be too cruel for me to give you a performance piece made up entirely from barre chords just yet. I'll reserve that particular torture for a little later on. For now though, here's a chord arrangement for you to practise with one lone barre in it. Try to ensure that forming the barre doesn't cause the rhythm to falter. It's far better to slow everything down so that your timing is on the button rather than allow long pauses to develop in your performance.

‖: A / / / |F#7 / / / | D / / / |E7 / / / :‖

SUMMARY

So let's take stock of what we have now in terms of barre chords. We have two shapes each for major, minor and dominant seventh chord – the three main chord families – and it's from these that we will complete our basic chord vocabulary.

Exactly how we do this is down to the barre chord system's big advantage over the other shapes you have learned: they move.

You might have noticed the little graphic on the barre chord diagrams pointing to something called the root. This is the note that gives the chord its name so, if we play a major barre here, with the root on the fifth fret, we have an A major chord:

NB: If the barre is too far up the neck to display the nut in the diagram, the thick horizontal line depicting the nut is not shown.

So, with a little bit of orienteering on the fretboard, it is possible for you to form all the major, minor and seventh chords you need. That's a huge step forward in forming your chord vocabulary.

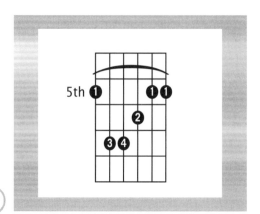

GOAL: TO RETURN TO THE SUBJECT OF MELODY AND LEARN HOW WE CAN INTEGRATE IT WITH CHORDS TO MAKE SONGS SOUND A LITTLE MORE 'CLASSY'.

MORE ACCOMPANIMENT IDEAS

I realise that you won't be able to take the fullest advantage of your new-found knowledge regarding barre chords until they fall under your fingers far more easily than they do now. So, for the moment, we'll take it that they represent your current 'work in progress' and that

you will have practised the shapes for when we begin to use them in a later Chapter.

NB: Incidentally, this sort of thing works fine with either pick or fingers so we won't have to worry about what side of the fence your preferences lie on in this respect.

WORKOUT 1

First of all, let's look at these chords. They're all shapes you know well.

At present, we have the choice of playing them four to the bar, eight to the bar, using combinations, leaving spaces, and so on. In fact, we've got quite a few accompaniment tools at our disposal, but there are other ways of linking chords together to give a smooth flow from one to the next.

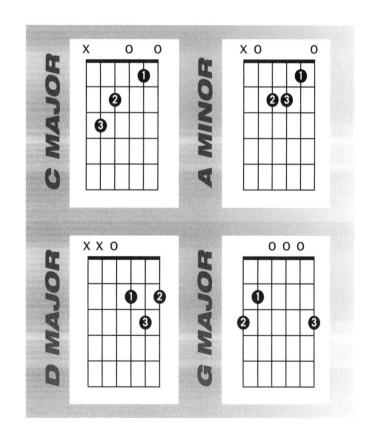

Take a look here:

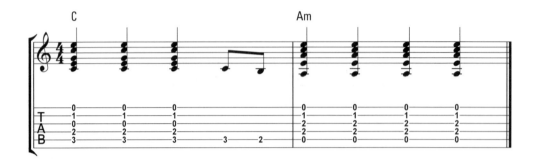

In the example above, the C major chord is partly strummed and partly picked to help it change into the A minor chord to good effect. This is useful for other transitions, too.

WORKOUT 2

Let's take another example:

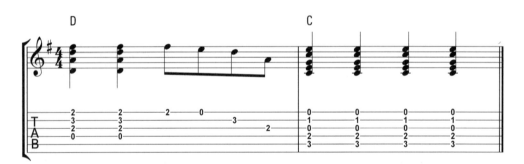

Here, we have a D major chord moving to C major with a few melody notes on the top strings to help things along. There's nothing extra to play: it's really just a case of lifting the fingers from the strings at the right time.

WORKOUT 3

Here's another case of two chords meeting each other
half way:

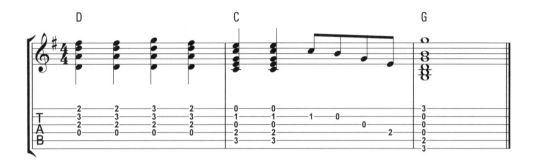

This is an arrangement using D major, C major and
G major chords with a little bit of melodic movement
in between them, so that they appear to gel together
a lot better. Naturally there is more than just the one
way of doing this. A lot of playing is down to an
individual player's taste, but in general, this is a widely
used method for getting around a chord arrangement.

One player who is very good at doing this sort of thing
is James Taylor. I'd recommend that you seek out some
of his recordings if you're not already familiar with his
material.

JAMES TAYLOR
*Singer-songwriter James Taylor's guitar style epitomises for many the best of the American folk
tradition, with clear, strong fingerpicking, sing-along strumming and a sprinkling of jazz thrown in.*

PERFORMANCE PIECE

So let's look at a long chord arrangement and see how we can tie the chords together a bit more to make everything sound 'whole'.

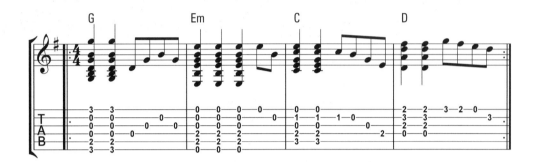

A lot of the elements contained in the example above will be unfamiliar to you, although I've tried to use chords that you've seen many times before. The idea is to practise each *change* individually – literally take everything in small bites – before you attempt a performance. When you're sure that everything is flowing smoothly, try it with the backing track.

SUMMARY

As you can see from this Chapter, chord changes aren't necessarily a matter of simply moving from one to the next. We can, in fact, be as ornate as we like, just as long as what we do actually suits the song in hand.

Try listening to as much acoustic guitar music as you can lay your hands on and hear what different players do with their chord changes. This way, you'll be learning when to play it straight and when to explore alternatives.

GOAL: TO UNDERSTAND THE VERSATILITY, IMPORTANCE, AND APPLICATION OF BARRE CHORDS.

BARRE CHORD EXTREME

How are the barre chords coming along?
Even if you've been putting in the practice
time, I expect that they are still feeling
awkward, but this isn't a problem.
This kind of thing won't come overnight,
but you will find that patient, persistent
practice will pay off and that things will
become much easier for you before long.

The best way to get the muscles in the hand built up
and ready to tackle barres is actually to use them as
much as possible. With this thought in mind, I thought
we'd do some basic orienteering lessons, finished off
with a whole piece made up entirely from barres!

JONI MITCHELL
Massively influential
and eminently listenable, Joni
Mitchell is the consummate
singer-songwriter, whose guitar
style is typified by non-
standard tunings that enable
her to use straightforward chord
shapes for some surprising –
and memorable – results.

WORKOUT 1

To begin with, let's review our stock of barre shapes:

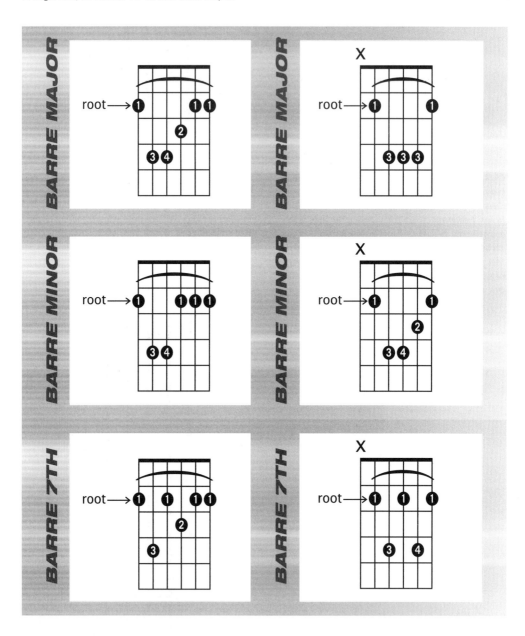

Six chords: two majors, two minors and two sevenths.
Now all we need to do is to learn to use them.

Take a look at the following chart:

This shows the names of the notes on the two lowest strings of your guitar. What I'd advise you to do is to copy this chart out onto a large piece of paper (A3 size is about right) and put it somewhere that guarantees you'll see it every day. On the back of a door, a bedroom wall, or anywhere in plain sight. The idea is that you begin to become familiar with the positions of the notes on the fretboard, at least for these two strings to begin with.

NB: In order to make the neck chart easier to read, the sharps and flats have been omitted. The note on the 4th fret of the E string can be called either G♯ (G sharp) or A♭ (A flat).

If you are having trouble remembering the in-between notes, refresh your memory by casting a glance at the chromatic scale on page 34.

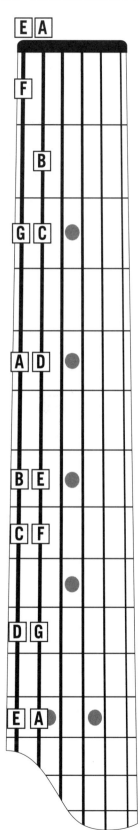

WORKOUT 2

The next thing to do is to learn how barre chords actually work. If you check the chord shapes below, you'll see that each has its root on the bass E string:

E-string roots

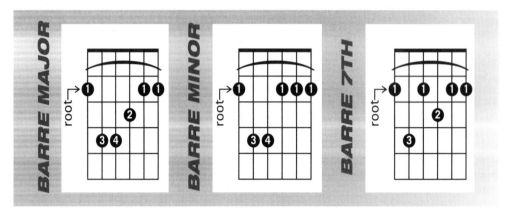

And the other group uses roots on the A:

A-string roots

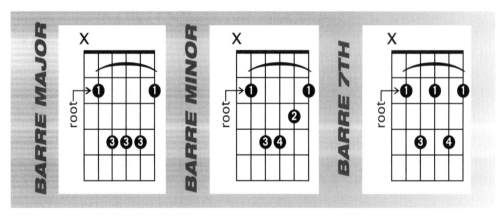

As I said in Chapter 17, it's the root note that gives us the name of the chord, so if we line the first group up with fret number eight – the note C – we get the following chords:

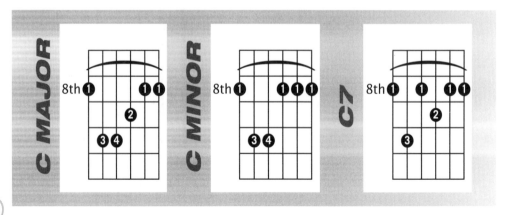

If we line them up with the note at the fourth fret, we get these:

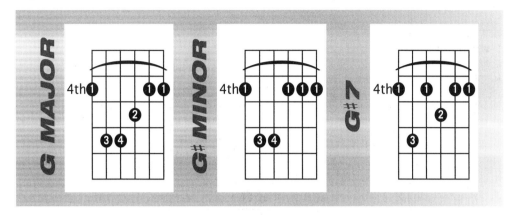

Now you might be beginning to see the value of learning barre shapes. We can get virtually all the chords we need from just a few shapes, simply by knowing where to put them.

WORKOUT 3

Let's try the same idea with the other group of barre shapes. First of all, we'll line them all up with the third fret on the A string.

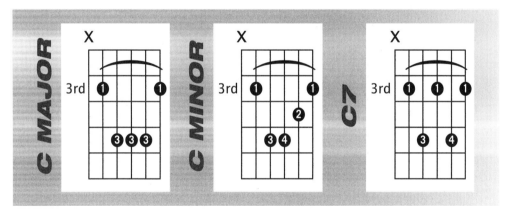

Once again, we've got C major, C minor and C7.

And if we move them up to the E at the seventh fret, we get E major, E minor and E7:

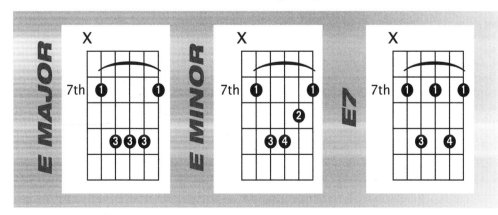

PERFORMANCE
PIECE

To finish this Chapter, I've constructed a chord arrangement which I want you to play using barre chords only. I've called it *Achy, Breaky Hand*.

| G / / / | G / / / | C / / / | D / / / |

| G / / / | G / / / | C / / / | D / / / |

| C / / / | D / / / | C / / / | D7 / / / |

| G / / / | G / / / | C / / / | D / / / |

| G / / / | G / / / ‖

SUMMARY

Moving the shapes around this way allows us full access to the basic pack of chords we need to make serious advances with playing. Now you can play all 36 and this will allow you to play literally hundreds of tunes. Of course, the hard work isn't over yet as it will take you a while to orientate yourself fully with the fretboard, and it's my guess that playing barre chords for longer than ten minutes is probably the limit for your left hand.

A good thing to add to your practice routine is a bit of 'note spotting' on the lower two strings. It needn't comprise anything more than finding one or two barres at random locations. Say to yourself 'B major' and find the chord using both the E and A string root variations. Gradually, you'll begin to remember where the notes/roots can be found and your chord vocabulary will begin to expand exponentially.

GOAL: TO INTRODUCE DYNAMICS, AND GET TO GRIPS WITH TONE.

DYNAMICS

Another element we have to process and be aware of when learning to play accompaniment on the guitar is dynamics. Quite literally, being able to play quietly, or really take the roof off.

You'll have noticed by now that your acoustic guitar doesn't have a volume control. Or, at least, it doesn't have an obvious volume control like a television. But this doesn't mean that we're not expected to put any dynamics into our playing. In fact far from it. The ability to vary the 'attack' in our playing is an important step towards being able to play with feeling, which is a vital element in music performance. So let's learn how it's done.

WORKOUT 1

Let's take a chord you know very well so that you don't have to worry too much about what the left hand is doing. For this job we need to concentrate on the right hand.

First of all, strike the strings with your pick or fingers the way you normally would. Now don't change a thing. This represents what we could call your 'standard dynamic'; well we could call it that if we wanted to be very pretentious, but you get the general idea. This is your 'centre notch' in terms of volume: the point from which you can play either louder or quieter. The idea now is to work out exactly how you can manipulate the strings to bring about a good, broad dynamic range.

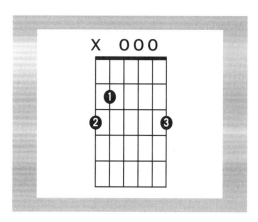

WORKOUT 2

The next job is to practise striking the strings with the pick or fingers incrementally in order to raise and lower the volume as you would if you actually had a volume control handy. Start with 'normal' and gradually reduce the amount of power you put behind your right hand. There will be a point where the guitar loses a lot of its tone and becomes very thin sounding and not at all attractive, and the trick is to know exactly where this point is and know how to stop just beforehand.

Next, we do exactly the same thing in the opposite direction; start at normal and work upwards in right-hand power. Once again, you're going to find that you reach a point where the guitar begins to sound harsh and unmusical. Make a mental note of where this point is and practise moving towards it, but never actually reaching it.

If you like, you can practise over a series of chords like these; begin quietly, become louder and then take the volume right back down towards the end.

|C / / / | C / / / |Am / / / | Am / / / |

|Dm / / / |Dm / / / |G7 / / / | C / / / ‖

WORKOUT 3

Now we're going to talk about tone. You might think that you haven't got an awful lot of control in this area either, but you're wrong. Try this: take another chord and strike it with your right hand in the place you would normally.

This means you should have struck the strings just to the right of the guitar's sound hole (from your perspective).

Now, move your right hand and strike the strings again nearer the bridge. It should sound a lot brighter. Naturally, you can't get too close to the bridge otherwise you end up with a really harsh and unmusical sound. Next, repeat the procedure by moving your hand towards the neck of the guitar. This time, you should hear the tone getting more mellow.

Make a note of the amount of 'useful' control you have in this area and experiment with it. You'll soon get to know where to strike the strings for the tone you require.

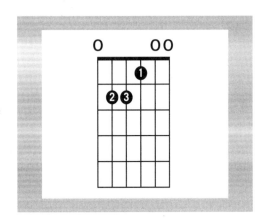

PERFORMANCE PIECE

So now you're aware of what you can do in the volume and tone areas, it's time to experiment with both these new parameters in your playing.

Here's a piece with which to practise your newly-acquired dynamic skills. Notice that I've put some recommendations in the music as to whether you should play it quiet, loud, sweet or brightly.

Tone: Bright (near bridge)
Volume: Loud

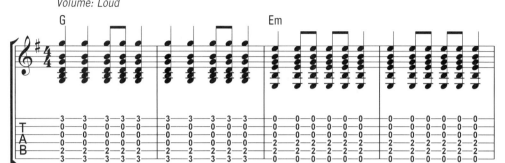

Getting quieter...

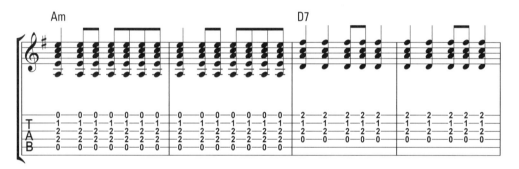

Sweet (near fretboard)
Quiet

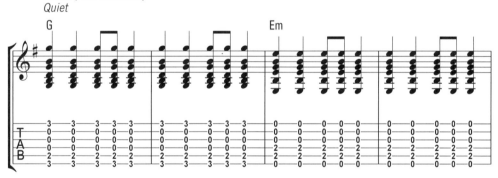

Getting louder...

Bright
Loud

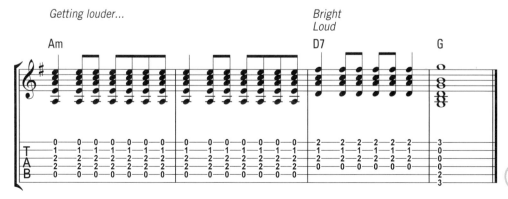

SUMMARY

An essential part of being an all-round guitarist is to be aware of exactly what parameters you have at your disposal in terms of volume and tone. This kind of knowledge sits beside your rudimentary skills of remembering chord shapes and barre positions, and adds to your overall performance immensely.

KIRK HAMMETT
Metallica's lead guitarist is held in high regard by his peers. The exercises studied in this chapter will stand you in good stead should you choose to transfer your skills to the dark side: electric rock.

GOAL: TO STREAMLINE YOUR PRACTICE TIME SO THAT YOU CAN BE SURE OF GETTING THE OPTIMUM AMOUNT OF GOOD FROM THE TIME YOU HAVE AVAILABLE.

STREAMLINING YOUR PRACTICE TIME

At this point in the book it would be wise for us to review everything you've done and put an efficient practice plan in place that will propel you forward. During all the years that I've been involved with teaching I've found that many practice schedules tend to be little more than groping around in the darkness, playing a few things over a couple of times and then shutting down shop. Wrong.

An effective plan must always contain challenging material that stands literally at the edge of your present capabilities in order to make progress possible. It all comes down to our unwillingness to face things we find difficult. It's human nature; but a good teacher will always push his students forward and test them at every turn. I can't actually stand behind you when you practise so you have to resolve to be very self-disciplined and try to keep the momentum flowing.

WORKOUT 1

The start of every session should be the same: first you need to make sure your guitar is in tune. Your ears should now be able to differentiate between an in-tune and an out-of-tune instrument, but we can't expect too much too soon, so checking the tuning with an electronic tuner is vital. The next job is to warm up, as you're asking muscles, tendons and so on to perform at their peak and we can't expect that from a standing start. I recommend some chord exercises like this one to begin with:

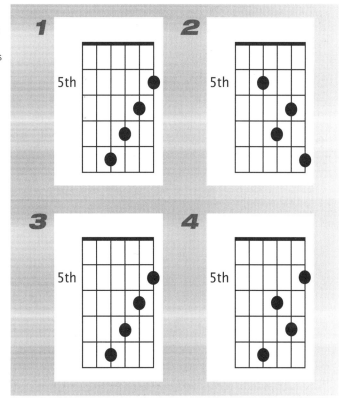

...or a simple scale exercise like this:

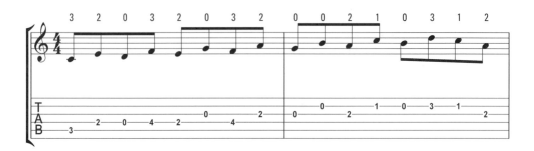

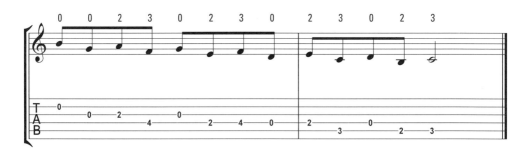

...anything that will gently stretch the fingers of both hands and prepare them for more demanding manoeuvres later on. You needn't spend too long warming up. Keep it proportionate to the amount of time you have to practise. Just a couple of minutes should be all that's necessary in the average 30-minute practice plan.

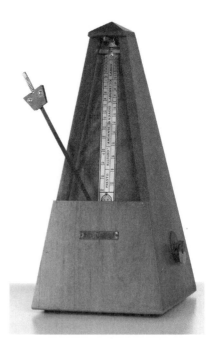

WORKOUT 2

After the warm up is complete, I think it's a good idea to continue with some scales and other co-ordination exercises. We looked at some scales earlier in the book and these will do fine. Just to keep some sort of edge to your playing, though, it's a good idea to practise using a metronome and increasing the speed gently as you progress.

Try this: here is a C major scale with no open strings in it...

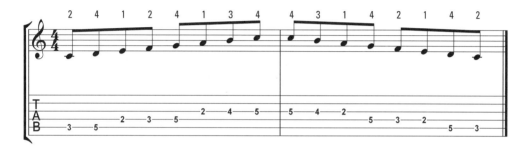

If you set your metronome to 60 beats per minute, practise playing one note per click. When you feel comfortable that this is working and is beginning to become effortless, turn the speed up slightly – no big leaps, as that would be missing the point – just enough to pose a challenge.

Then, when everything settles down a bit, increase the speed again, and so on. Be very strict with yourself, though, it's no good ploughing forward if the scale is falling apart or notes are beginning to drift off time. Be patient and expect the process of speeding up to take weeks rather than days.

The next part of your practice session should represent 'work in progress'. You can vary this from day to day. You have enough material from this book alone to make sure that you don't end up doing the exact same thing for weeks on end, but don't vary things too much.

Set aside some time for working on problems, too. We all have them: a tricky chord change or a fingering that never seems to go right; this is the time to iron out the wrinkles. If you've got a bad chord change in one of the songs, don't practise it by playing through the whole thing; just sit there for a few minutes and practise the part causing the problem. This is time-efficient and a good way of ironing out the lumps in your playing.

At the end of your practice session, go through the things you can play well. This is the time to keep your repertoire polished up.

It's also time to have fun, too: it's very easy to lose sight of the fact that playing music is meant to be an enjoyable experience so always make time to play through something you know well and enjoy doing it.

PERFORMANCE PIECE

To end this Chapter, here are a few exercises to play through to keep those fingers busy. Each of them is a deliberate 'twister' that will test you a little, but you can rest assured that it's doing you a lot of good at the same time.

This might not sound quite as musical as some of the other performance pieces, but it's doing you a lot of good.

Repeat each exercise five times

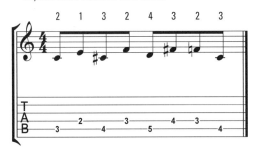

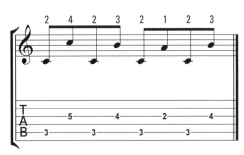

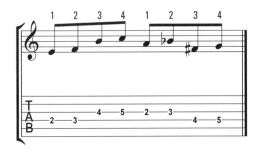

SUMMARY

There is a great deal of benefit to be gained from organising your practice sessions. Ideally, it should be run almost like a military campaign with as little of that most valuable of resources – your time – wasted as possible. You also need to be sure that what you're doing is of maximum benefit to you and that your learning is progressive and never stagnant. What I've detailed above is a way of ensuring your time in this respect is well spent. The rest, as they say, is up to you.

GOAL: *HERE WE ARE GOING TO TAKE ANOTHER LOOK AT THE BLUES AND WORK ON HOW TO PLAY SOME GOOD-SOUNDING MELODY OVER THE TOP OF A 12-BAR BLUES IN E.*

BLUES YOU CAN USE
It would be difficult to overstate the influence that blues has had on popular music. The blues is everywhere: in jazz, country, rock, pop... you name it. It's such a common denominator in music that avoiding it is nigh on impossible. We've already learnt a little bit about the blues, so let's look a little bit deeper.

In order to do this, we need two things: a chord chart and a new scale. So before we do anything else, let's look at the chart.

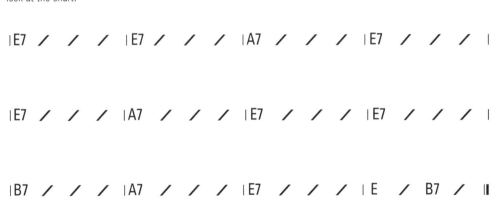

WORKOUT 1

First of all, let's consider the chords themselves.
By now, you should be beginning to remember these
shapes, but just in case, here's a crib sheet:

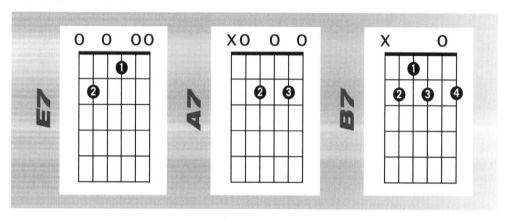

All of these shapes we dealt with a while ago so there
shouldn't really be a problem with changing between
them, but go ahead and try each chord change
individually to make sure that you are moving smoothly
from one to the next.
There's the E7 to the A7:

**Finger 2 hops over to
the D string.**

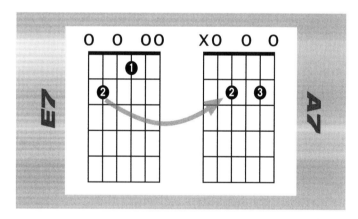

And back again:

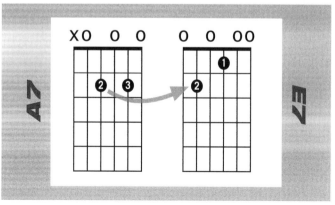

WORKOUT 2

Now the E7 to B7:

Finger 2 remains in position while finger 1 hops back a string.

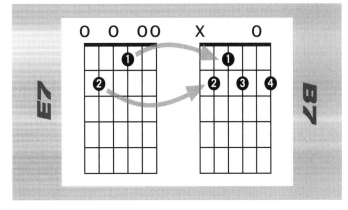

And the B7 to A7:

Fingers 2 and 3 move together in formation.

And that just about covers the whole thing.

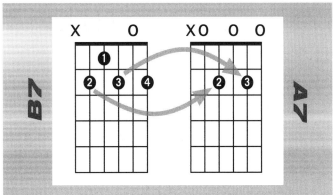

WORKOUT 3

The only other glitch that you might come across is the final bar where you have to change between the E7 and B7 quite quickly. If we take this bar independently, it looks like this:

| E7   /   B7   / ||

So you would count through it like this:

| E7   /   B7   / ||
  1   2   3   4

In other words, there are two beats on the E7 and two on the B7. In order to make sure that this is no problem, practise it now and get it out of the way. Don't play through the rest of the chords, just isolate this one change and play it through until it begins to feel right.

The idea of changing chords 'two to the bar' is far from uncommon in music, sometimes they even change on every beat, so beware. It might sound scary, but it's nothing you won't be able to deal with once your chord-wrangling skills are up to scratch.

WORKOUT 4

Once you can play through the chords slowly but cleanly, it's time to move on to the next part of the Chapter: a little bit of blues lead guitar, no less. As we've seen before, blues is a very characteristic sound so it's no surprise that it has its own scale. This one, in fact:

It even sounds bluesy on its own, without any chords underneath, but there's more good news to come, because this particular scale fits our blues in E like a glove. It's quite easy to make it sound 'right' over the top of the chords, as you can see from the DVD.

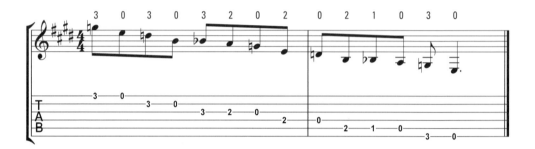

PERFORMANCE
PIECE

All I am asking you to do here is to practise the blues scale over the backing track and have some fun with it. You'll be surprised at how easy it is to make the scale sound like a reasonable guitar solo, even when your choice of notes is fairly random.

Here once again is the chord chart that is being played by the backing track:

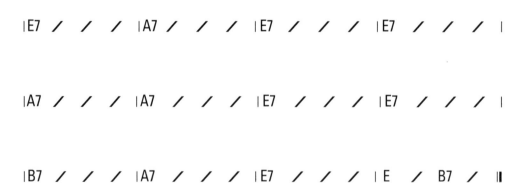

And here's your scale:

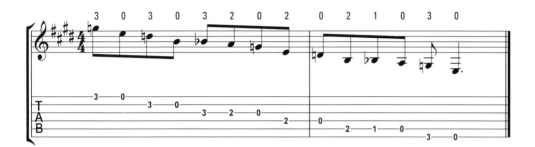

As your ear develops you will find that you become more and more selective and, who knows, we might make a blues player out of you yet.

SUMMARY

In this Chapter we've looked at the blues as a more complete package. In other words, you now have an idea about what a 12-bar blues is all about from the point of view of both harmony and melody. You've also taken your first few steps into the world of improvisation.

GOAL: TO LOOK AT THE STRANDS OF LEARNING WE HAVE ALREADY PUT TOGETHER AND CONSIDER HOW THEY CONTINUE, BEGINNING WITH CHORDS.

FUTURE STUDY

Now that we are approaching the end of your lesson plan, it's time to look into the future and see what lies ahead of you in terms of continuing your learning. I've tried to be as comprehensive as I can be and I've made sure that you're aware of all of the essentials as far as the fundamentals are concerned. For instance, you should be able to work your way through a lot of songs now, playing a good rhythmic accompaniment with the occasional flourish in there, too.

WORKOUT 1

Remember when I said that the basic starter pack of chords comprises 36? That's 12 majors, 12 minors and 12 dominant sevenths, but there are many more variations, as you've probably come across yourself by looking though sheet music. It might seem a little bit bewildering, but all the chords you don't yet know can be looked at as mere variations on the ones you do, so let's look at how that works.

To begin with, let's take the major family. So far, you're familiar with the basic major chord formed from every note of the chromatic scale. The 'mother scale' in music made up from 12 notes. However, you are going to come across these variations:

Major 7
Major 6
Major 9
Major 6/9

The good news here is that all of the above variations are based on something you already know. As an example, let's look at a couple of C chords.

On the left is the chord you already know, C major. On the left is C major7. To begin with, play both and listen hard; they should sound similar. Then look at the diagrams again. See the difference between the two? It's one note, that's all; in fact all that is happening here is that we've added another note to the basic major chord in order to add a bit of 'colour', nothing more.

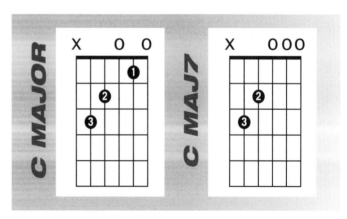

The C major7 sounds a little sweeter as a result, but it's still basically a C major chord. In other words, if you see a 'major 7' chord in a songbook and you're unsure what to do with it, you wouldn't actually be doing anything wrong if you just played the straight major chord of the same name instead. In other words, instead of D major7, you play D major. It won't sound dead right, but it certainly won't be wrong, and furthermore, I'd be very surprised if anyone listening to you even notices.
This goes for any of the other variations in the list above, too, so you could think like this:

For C6, C major6/9, C major9 etc. play C major, and so on.

WORKOUT 2

Believe it or not, this works for the other families, too. You'll come across chord symbols belonging to the dominant family like these:

C9
C13
C7/6

Once again, compare these two chords:

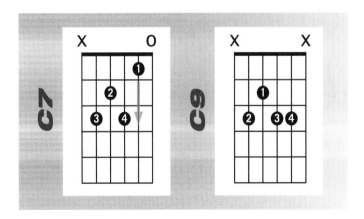

Sound similar, don't they? So the same rule applies; all you have to do is to play a C7 instead and all will be well. Of course, I'm not recommending this as a code of practice; I would actually encourage you to learn the chords you don't know by trial and error. In other words, if you come across something you don't know, look it up. If you're in the middle of playing and can't put the guitar down and reach for your chord book, use a substitute like I've suggested above.

WORKOUT 3

It's probably no surprise that the substitution rule applies to the minor family of chords, too:

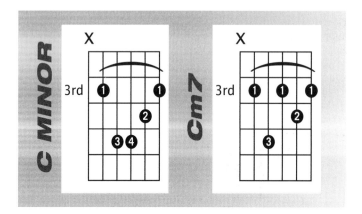

Again, they don't sound exactly the same, but they sound similar enough to use in an emergency. The worst thing you can do is to mix up the chord families and use a major chord instead of a minor or a dominant instead of a major. As long as you can sort out which family an unknown chord is from, you should be OK. The only chords to watch out for are these:

Sus chords
Diminished chords
Augmented chords

Here, you will have to look them up as there really are no substitutes available to you in the short term. Luckily, none of the above types crop up for more than half a bar or so at a time at the most so you won't be caught out too often.

SCALES

There are other scales in music, loads of them in fact. All I've done so far is give you the most common one: the major scale. But there are 12 major scales, one for each key, and the pros know them all.

There are dominant scales and minor scales to consider, too, and that's only the tip of the iceberg. The good news here is that if you intend to play an accompanying role with your guitar – playing rhythm underneath a song or something – then scales aren't going to be too important to you. If you're aiming at the virtuoso league, they're vital.

Obviously I haven't got the space to show you all the scales, but there are plenty of books on the market that will take you wherever you want to go as far as melody is concerned so the information is out there and yours for the asking.

PERFORMANCE PIECE

In conclusion, though, here are four scales to look at.
Listen to the sound they make against the backing
provided – they all work against the one track – and hear
how a little further investigation into the world of melody
on your part can take you a long way.

C dominant scale

C natural minor scale

C minor pentatonic scale

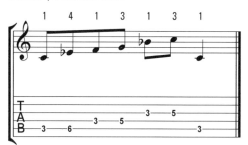

C major pentatonic scale

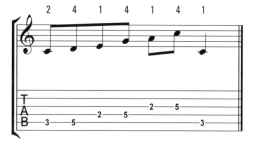

SUMMARY

*In order to make the best possible use
of the material we've covered in this
book, you have to engage in a little lateral
thinking. You've seen how building a
good-sized chord vocabulary enables
you to play more and more pieces, and
it's the same with scales and melody.
I'd encourage you to root out as much
information as you can in both these
areas and enrich the knowledge you've
already gained.*

GOAL: *TO LOOK AT THE SONG, WORK OUT WHICH CHORD SHAPES YOU'RE GOING TO BE USING AND MAKE SURE THAT THEY ARE ALL AS CLOSE TO EACH OTHER ON THE NECK AS POSSIBLE.*
TO WORK ON THE RHYTHM OF THE SONG AND COME UP WITH AN INTRODUCTION.

GRAND FINALE

It's Graduation Day! For this final Chapter, we're going to look at a whole song from scratch which you will end up performing against a specially-written backing track that has been designed to make your acoustic guitar playing sound fabulous, but I'm going to make you work for it.

WORKOUT 1

To begin with, here's the basic chart you're going to be following:

There are no chords here that you don't know, but I have put in one or two barre chords just to challenge you a little. The thing to do here is to work through the chart,

play through the changes and make sure your fingers know their way around before going any further. If you really get lost at any point, check out the DVD where we go through the chart, showing you where the best chord positions are to be found.

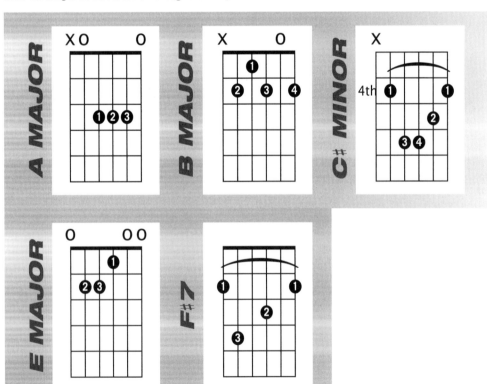

WORKOUT 2

Next, we'll work through some rhythmic ideas. Obviously we don't want to keep changing the strum pattern all the time as one of the principal roles of rhythm guitar is just that: rhythm. So it helps push the song along if your strum pattern remains consistent. Here are a couple of ideas:

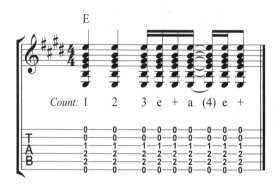

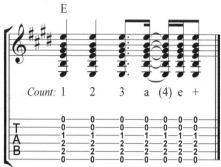

WORKOUT 3

Now let's look at the intro. I've tried to keep your part as simple as possible (you've already got a lot to think about) but there are some 'bluesy' notes for you to play along with the guitar on the backing track.
Here they are:

Intro:

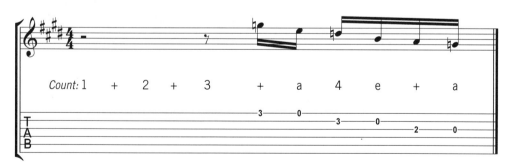

PERFORMANCE PIECE

Here is the complete piece to work on. Remember to take things slowly and only work on small sections at any one time. If you work on the song in these three distinct areas – chords, rhythm and intro – you will be best prepared for the final challenge; performing the song itself over the audio track.

Remember to take everything slowly – bite-size chunks and definitely not the whole thing all at once – and then, when you're absolutely sure that you've got everything up and running, it's time for a performance. Good luck.

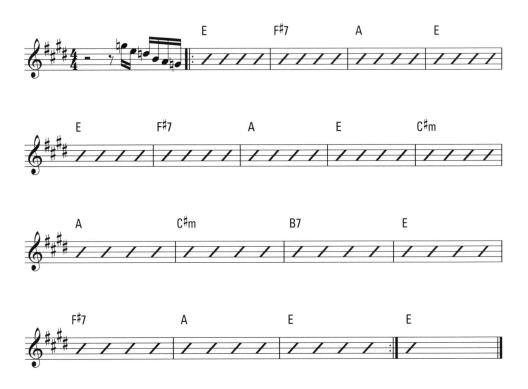

SUMMARY

You've come a long way since the start of the book; from those ambling first chords to a full-sounding performance piece. We've covered a lot of ground and covered it quickly. I hope that you've gained a lot from working through these Chapters and that you will continue your studies, learning more about chords, scales, rhythm and everything you need to know in order to become a master guitarist.

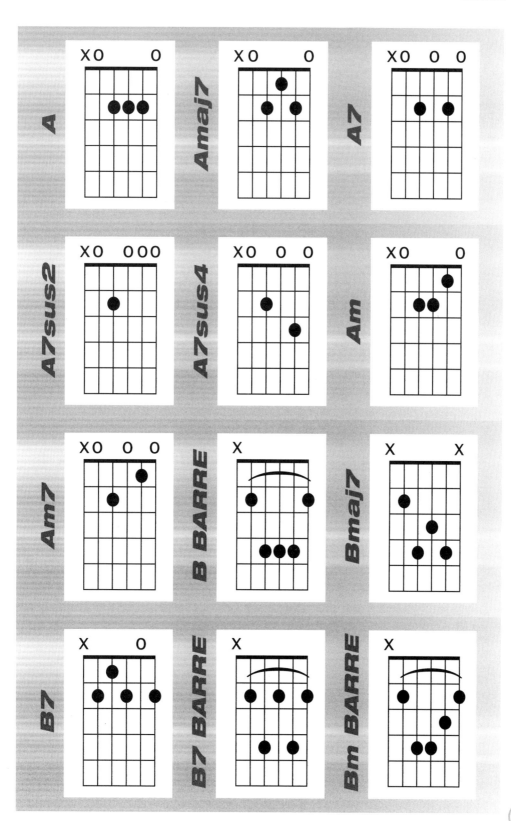

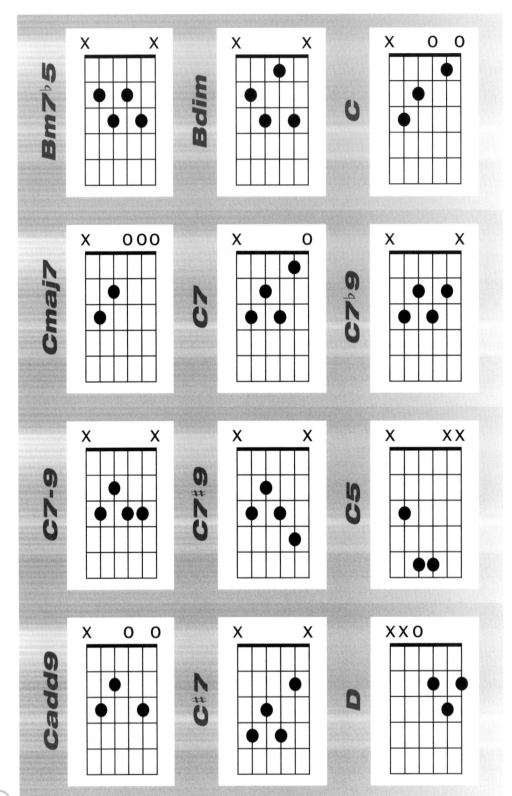

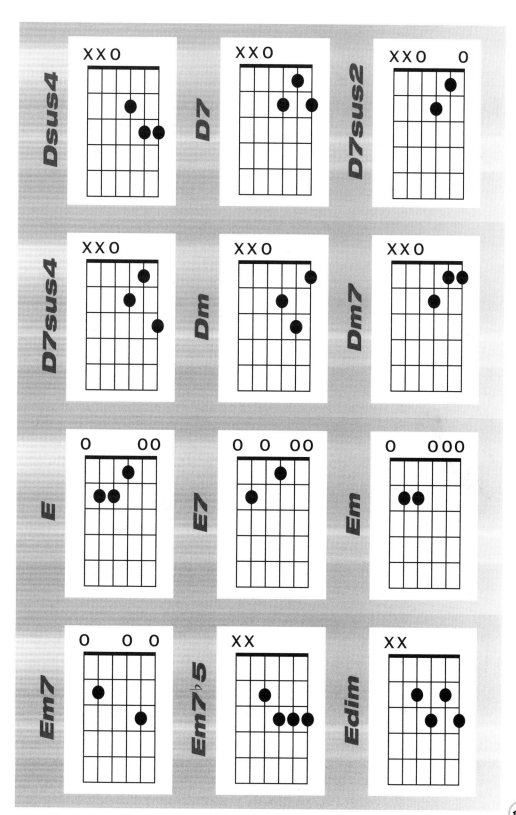

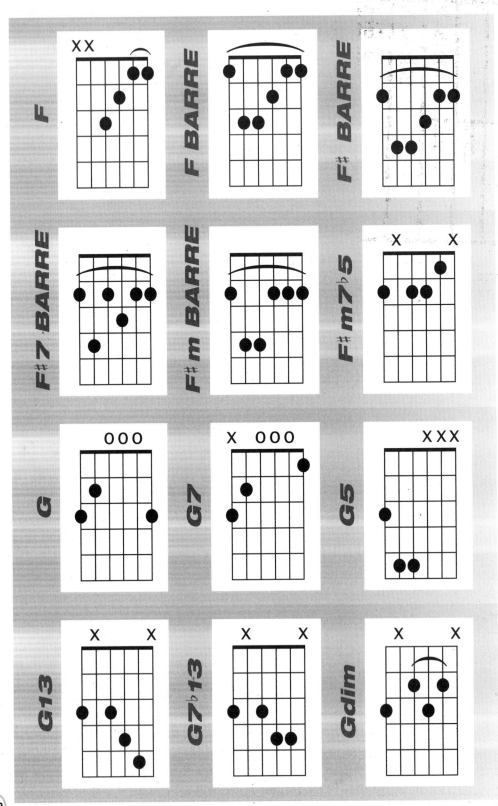

1/13(185770)